# EATING FOR LIFE
## A BOOK ABOUT VEGETARIANISM

In this timely and relevant book, a young man looks at the subject of vegetarianism in a cool, clear and logical way. He has drawn on material from many sources, particularly those that are objective and scientific and have no vested interest in the vegetarian movement. This book is well documented and is presented in a concise, easy-to-read format. Not only from the moral and humane standpoints, but from the points of view of man's anatomy and physiology, of health and nutrition, of the world food shortage and ecology, the case for vegetarianism is made clear. There is also much helpful information on food values and what to eat in place of meat.

Nathaniel Altman was born in 1948 in New York City, and graduated from the University of Wisconsin. He was raised as a meat eater but became a vegetarian at the age of twenty-one when he was studying in Latin America. He says that he decided to stop eating meat when he learned that man's violence toward the animals is related to the wars he wages with his own kind. At the age of twenty-three he decided to find out more about the subject of vegetarianism, and this book is the result.

# EATING FOR LIFE

## A BOOK ABOUT
## VEGETARIANISM

Nathaniel Altman

A QUEST BOOK ORIGINAL

THE THEOSOPHICAL PUBLISHING HOUSE
Wheaton, Ill., U.S.A.
Madras, India / London, England

The Theosophical Publishing House, Wheaton, Illinois,
    is a department of The Theosophical Society in America

Altman, Nathaniel, 1948-
    Eating for life.

    (A Quest book original)
    Bibliography: p.
    1. Vegetarianism.   I. Title.
TX392.A53                    641.5'636                    73-1950
ISBN  0-8356-0437-3

Manufactured in the United States of America

This book is dedicated to

Guillermo Neira
Edgar Brecci

and to my younger brothers the animals,
on whose behalf this book was written.

# CONTENTS

# ACKNOWLEDGMENTS

The author gratefully acknowledges permission to use material from the following individuals and corporations:

The University of Chicago Press, Chicago, Illinois for information quoted from pages 239, 249, and 250 of *The Vertebrate Story* by A. S. Romer;

Fearn Soya Foods, Melrose Park, Illinois for material obtained from their Composition of Foods chart;

Mrs. Frances Moore Lappé, for use of the Protein Cost Comparisons chart found on pages 272-4 of *Diet for a Small Planet*;

Rodale Books Inc., Emmaus, Pennsylvania for their Vitamin E chart found on page 349 of *The Complete Book of Vitamins*;

Mrs. Mattie Louise Gephardt for three recipes from her book *Recipes for Vegetarians*;

Natural Hygiene Press, Chicago, Illinois for the chart of comparative anatomy taken from *Fit Food for Man* by A. D. Andrews, Jr.;

The MacMillan Co. for information quoted from pages 115, 155, 286, and 289 of *Foundations of Nutrition,* sixth edition, by C. M. Taylor and O. F. Pye, 1966.

The writer also acknowledges with gratitude the valued assistance of Victoria Mucie, who took part in the principal stages of research, editing, proofreading, and typing. Deep thanks also go to those of the headquarters staff at the Theosophical Society in America who generously gave of their time and energy in the research, criticism, and proofreading of the manuscript. Many other individuals deserve thanks for their ideas, information and opinions which have been of great value to the author.

Finally the author acknowledges with sorrow the suffering and death of the animals sacrificed in laboratory research which produced some of the findings presented herein.

N.A.

# INTRODUCTION

## COMPASSION: THE HEART OF THE VEGETARIAN PHILOSOPHY AND WAY OF LIFE

The Sanskrit word for compassion is *Ahimsa,* meaning "harmlessness" or not hurting. This quality is regarded as one of very great importance since it is believed that the first step in the regeneration of man must be to eliminate cruelty. Therefore wise sages prescribed *Ahimsa* which was regarded by them as the most effective master-method to counteract and eradicate the brutal, cruel tendencies in man.

The practice of *Ahimsa* develops universal love which is pure love. Where there is *Ahimsa* there is compassion and selfless service. *Ahimsa* is said to be the noblest and best of traits that are found expressed in the daily life and activities of perfected beings. *Ahimsa* is the one sure means to attain salvation for mankind and to enjoy uninterrupted peace and bliss; for man attains peace by injuring no living creature.

Actually, it is taught, there is but one religion—the religion of love, of true kindness, of peace. There is but one message, the message of *Ahimsa* which is the highest duty of man. *Ahimsa,* or refraining from causing pain to any living creature, is thus a distinctive quality emphasized by Indian ethics and has been the central doctrine of Indian culture from the earliest days of its history. Throughout that time *Ahimsa,* or nonviolence, has proved to be a great spiritual force.

*Ahimsa* or noninjury naturally implies nonkilling and is therefore at the heart of the vegetarian philosophy of life. Noninjury is not merely nonkilling, however. In its comprehensive meaning, noninjury means entire abstinence from causing any pain or harm whatsoever to any living creature, either by thought, word, or deed. Noninjury demands a harmless mind, mouth, and hands. Thus *Ahimsa* is not mere negative noninjury; it is positive Cosmic Love. It arises from development of the mental attitude in which hatred is replaced by love.

The need is most urgent. A deep disharmony exists in the world and it is being continually deepened. Horrid discord reigns on earth. Uncountable millions of human beings and many more millions of animals have suffered, now suffer, and inevitably will suffer and die unnecessarily, in great pain and at tremendous financial cost. A state of emergency exists as world statistics of premature mortality, disease, famine, and "accident" unmistakably demonstrate. Bloodguilt and bloodstain must be removed from the conscience, soul and life of man. As long as cruelty persists, spiritual progress is retarded, spiritual activity hampered, and every reform is delayed by obstacles created by man himself.

Individual humaneness, vegetarianism, and healthy living are magnificent first steps towards a solution of this world problem. Active societies advocating these three essentials to health and happiness render far-reaching service to the human race. Means must immediately be found to strengthen them and to increase their effectiveness. The gospels of humaneness, food reform, and the healthy life must be spread throughout the whole world with ever greater diligence and efficiency. Totality of attack is, I submit, urgently demanded.

The inculcation of humaneness must especially be accepted as an essential part of education. The child must have kindness and cooperation, not cruelty and competition, insistently taught by example and precept at home and at school. Humane education will produce a humane humanity. Humanitarianism is essential to world peace and human health and happiness and should be taught in every school and college. For unless it brings these blessings, what is the value of education? In the coming Age, it is proclaimed, world unity, world cooperation, and world-wide humaneness will be accepted ideals.

I am privileged to contribute an introduction to this book on vegetarianism so ably presented by my valued friend, Nathaniel Altman.

GEOFFREY HODSON,
Vice-President
International Vegetarian Union

# PREFACE

Although thousands of years old, man's natural diet has been slandered, ridiculed, and feared by people throughout the ages. And despite its proven economy, nutritional benefits, and harmlessness towards life, the vegetarian diet has been largely ignored in the West in favor of one containing meat.

The purpose of this book is to introduce the lay reader to the subject of the meat free diet, whether the reader be a meat eater, or a practicing vegetarian. The author feels that the acceptance or rejection of a vegetarian diet should not be based on emotion, conditioning, prejudice, or hearsay, but on the careful consideration of the facts of the matter, and an intelligent decision which is based on the truth.

In this spirit, the author has attempted to incorporate facts taken largely from objective scientific sources which do not have a vested interest in the vegetarian movement. Every fact and quote presented in this book includes the source from which the information was taken.

It is hoped that this book will serve as a useful tool in the individual's quest for truth, and facilitate the sharing of this knowledge with others.

NATHANIEL ALTMAN
Ojai, California
December, 1972

# Chapter 1

# HISTORY OF VEGETARIANISM

"Thou shalt not kill."
— The Holy Commandments

Man's involvement with a vegetarian diet appears to extend as far back as life itself, since there is no anthropological evidence that man evolved through flesh-eating animals. Recent scientific investigations have found that modern man's early ancestors were basically vegetarians who ate no meat except during periods of extreme crisis. In the book *Early Man,* author F. Clark Howell writes:

> The massive jaw, heavy skull musculature, and huge molar teeth of Paranthropus (primitive man) lead some investigators to conclude that he was essentially a vegetarian. This idea is further supported by the fact that in Southern Africa the brownish breccias yielding Paranthropus remains indicate that a moister climate and, as a result, a richer and more densely vegetated habitat may have prevailed than exists there today. In such an ecological situation— and with his dental equipment—it seems likely that Paranthropus would have existed largely, as some apes still do, on green shoots, edible leaves and seasonal fruits and nuts of various kinds, only rarely seeking out small game.[1]

The Ice Age is recognized as the principal factor that forced early Homo sapiens to revert to the eating of animal flesh in order to survive. This custom of meat eating has continued throughout the history of mankind, either by necessity (as in the case of the Eskimo) or through habit, conditioning, or lack of knowledge, as is the case of most meat eaters today.

From the beginnings of recorded history we find that vegetarianism was regarded as the natural diet of man.

In the *Encyclopaedia of Religion and Morals* we find:

> Ancient Egypt and Greece knew the religious form
> of vegetarianism, and their myths, like the earliest
> Hebrew, represented man as having been originally
> a fruit eating creature.[2]

In ancient Greece such figures as Plato[3], Diogenes[4], and
the great mathematician and sage Pythagoras[5] were out-
spoken advocates of a nonmeat diet. In India, the Buddha
stressed the doctrine of Ahimsa — harmlessness to all living things. "For fear of causing terror to living beings . . .
let the Bodhisattva who is disciplining himself to attain
compassion, refrain from eating flesh."[6] Today many of
his 400 million followers are strict vegetarians, especially
the priests. In early Roman times, such men as Seneca[7],
Virgil[8], Ovid[9], and the poet Horace[10] advocated and prac-
ticed the vegetarian way of living.

The Bible clearly states in Genesis I:29 what the natural
diet of man was intended to be:

> And God said, "Behold, I have given you every
> herb bearing seed, which is upon the face of all the
> earth, and every tree, in the which is the fruit of a
> tree yielding seed; to you it shall be for meat."[11]

Abstention from flesh food was further decreed in Genesis IX:4:

> But flesh with the life thereof, which is the blood
> thereof, shall ye not eat.[12]

The Epistle of St. Paul to the Romans reflects a similar
idea.

> It is good neither to eat flesh . . . nor any thing
> whereby thy brother stumbleth, or is offended, or is
> made weak.[13]          Romans XIV:21

*The Essene Gospel of Peace,* a direct translation of early
Aramaic texts, recounts the words of Jesus Christ in regard to this subject:

> And the flesh of slain beasts in his body will be-
> come his own tomb. For I tell you truly, he who kills,

kills himself, and whoso eats the flesh of slain beasts, eats the body of death.[14]

Other ancient religious writings reflect similar positions on the eating of meat. The Vedic book of wisdom, the *Laws of Manu,* states:

> Meat can never be obtained without injury to living creatures, and injury to sentient beings is detrimental to [the attainment of] heavenly bliss; let him therefore shun [the use of] meat.[15]

In *The Essential Unity of All Religions,* Bhagavan Das writes:

> Ali, nephew and son-in-law of Muhammed, and said to be the first Sufi in Islam after the Prophet himself, is reported as having advised the higher aspirants: "Make not your stomachs graves for animals."[16]

This position is also reflected in The Koran, the holy book of the Islamic faith:

> The Qur'an (Koran) prohibits the eating of 'what is dead, and blood, and flesh of swine, and whatsoever has been consecrated to other than God.'[17]

Throughout history we find that many of the world's most outstanding writers, artists, scientists, philosophers, and teachers have been enthusiastic advocates of and adherents to a meat-free diet. Some of these individuals include Plutarch[18], Porphyry[19], William Shakespeare[20], Leonardo Da Vinci[21], Sir Isaac Newton[22], Jean Jacques Rousseau[23], Francois Voltaire[24], Benjamin Franklin[25], Charles Darwin[26], Richard Wagner[27], Gen. William Booth[28], Ralph Waldo Emerson[29], Henry David Thoreau[30], Percy Bysshe Shelley[31], Dr. J. H. Kellogg[32], Alexander Pope[33], Rabindranath Tagore[34], Leo Tolstoy[35], Upton Sinclair[36], H. G. Wells[37], Albert Einstein[38], Dr. Annie Besant[39], George Bernard Shaw[40], Gen. George Montgomery[41], Albert Schweitzer[42], Mahatma Gandhi[43], J. Krishnamurti[44], and His Holiness the Dalai Lama of Tibet.[45]

In all fairness, it should be mentioned that there is some evidence that Adolf Hitler abstained from meat eating for several years, in the hope of achieving greater stamina and a longer life through a vegetarian diet. Regarding Hitler's vegetarianism, H. Jay Dinshah writes: "No one has ever claimed that vegetarianism was a sure cure for insanity and surely we may be allowed a single rotten apple in even the finest barrel of good fruit."[46]

Many religions, as well as other spiritual and science-oriented groups (or members of those groups) have advocated, officially or unofficially, a vegetarian diet for either health, ethical, or religious reasons. Such organizations and religious bodies include The Theosophical Society; The Adventist Church; the Essene, Hindu, Buddhist, Zoroastrian, Tao, and Jain faiths; the Unity Church; the Order of the Cross; the Liberal Catholic Church; the Vegan Society; The American Natural Hygiene Society; the Trappist, St. Benedict, and Carthusian orders of the Roman Catholic Church, as well as other Christian organizations such as the Universal Christian Gnostic Movement and the Rosicrucian Fellowship.

## The Vegetarian Movement

Shortly after the introduction of the term "vegetarian" in 1842, the first independent organization devoted to advocating a fleshless diet was formed in England in the year 1847. In 1871, forty-one members of the Bible Christian Church sailed from England to settle in Philadelphia, where their number soon increased. Their philosophy was strengthened through the influence of such men as Dr. Rueben D. Mussey (fourth president of the American Medical Association), and the Rev. Sylvester Graham, whose research in grains led to the use of Graham flour for baking. The pioneer of the breakfast food industry, J. H. Kellogg, M.D., was also a strict vegetarian and one of the most enthusiastic supporters of the vegetarian movement in America.

The world's largest vegetarian organization, the International Vegetarian Union, was founded in 1908, and at the present time comprises branches throughout the world. In the United States there are two principal organizations which promote vegetarianism from the standpoints of both health and morality: The American Vegetarian Union, and the American Vegan Society. It is estimated that the total number of vegetarians in the United States lies between 2.5 and 3 million people.[47]

The past few years have witnessed a groundswell of interest both in natural foods and especially in the vegetarian diet, predominantly among the young. From all indications, such interest will continue to spread as more people learn that vegetarianism is not merely a passing fad, but a proven, inexpensive, humane, healthful and practical way of living.

### References

[1]Howell, F. Clark; *Early Man*; Time-Life Books, New York, 1965, pp. 66-7
[2]Hastings, James, ed.; *Encyclopaedia of Religion and Morals*; Vol. VI, Charles Scribner's Sons, New York, p. 62
[3]*The Encyclopaedia Britannica*; Vol. 22, Encyclopedia Britannica Inc., Chicago, 1967, p. 935
[4]*Ibid.*
[5]Ovid; *Metamorphoses*; Indiana University Press, Bloomington, 1958, pp. 367-9
[6]Suzuki, D. T.; *Lankavatara Sutra*; George Routledge and Sons Ltd., London, 1932, p. 213
[7]*Encyclopaedia Britannica; op. cit.*
[8]Hardinge, M. G. and Crooks, H.; "Non-Flesh Dietaries;" *Journal of the American Dietetic Association*; Vol. 43, No. 6, December 1963, p. 546
[9]*Metamorphoses; op. cit.*
[10]*Non-Flesh Dietaries; op. cit.*
[11]*The Holy Bible*; Thomas Nelson & Sons, p. 2
[12]*Ibid.*, p. 8
[13]*Ibid.*, p. 163
[14]Szekely, Edmond Bordeaux, trans.; *The Essene Gospel of Peace*; Academy of Creative Living, San Diego, 1970, p. 44
[15]Buhler, G., trans.; *The Laws of Manu*; Motilal Banarsidass, Delhi, 1967, Vol. 48, p. 176
[16]Das, Bhagavan; *The Essential Unity of All Religions*; The Theosophical Publishing House (Quest Book), Wheaton, Illinois, 1966, pp. 472-3
[17]*Encyclopaedia of Religion and Morals; op. cit.*

[18]*Encyclopaedia Americana*; Vol. 27, Americana Corporation, New York, 1962, p. 720

[19]Seyffert, Oskar, ed.; *Dictionary of Classical Antiquities*; The World Publishing Co., Cleveland, 1966, p. 505

[20]Shakespeare, William; *Henry VI*, Part 2, Act 3, Scene 2, Line 188; Great Books of the Western World, Vol. 26; Encyclopaedia Britannica Inc., Chicago, 1952, p. 53

[21]Da Vinci, Leonardo; *Selections from the Notebooks of Leonardo Da Vinci*; Oxford University Press, London, 1952, p. 375

[22]*Encyclopaedia Britannica, op. cit.*

[23]*Ibid.*

[24]*Non-Flesh Dietaries; op. cit.*

[25]Franklin, Benjamin; *The Autobiography of Benjamin Franklin*; The Modern Library, New York, p. 20

[26]Darwin, Charles; *The Descent of Man*; D. Appleton & Co., New York, 1890, p. 156

[27]Freshel, M. R. L., ed.; *Selections from Three Essays by Richard Wagner*; The Millenium Guild Inc., Rochester, N.H., 1933, p. 19

[28]Arundale, Rukmini Devi, *et al.*; *The Vegetarian Way*; The Indian Vegetarian Congress, Madras, 1967, p. 155

[29]*Harper's Magazine*; March 1970, p. 91

[30]Canby, H. S.; *Thoreau*; Houghton Mifflin Co., Boston, 1939, p. 36

[31]Clark, D. L., ed.; *Shelley's Prose*; University of New Mexico Press, 1954, Albuquerque, 1954, pp. 81-90

[32]*Journal of the American Dietetic Association; op. cit.*, p. 547

[33]Boynton, H. W., ed.; *The Complete Works of Pope*; Houghton Mifflin Co., Boston, 1931, p. 139

[34]*The Vegetarian Way; op. cit.*, p. 141

[35]Spence, Gordon W.; *Tolstoy, the Ascetic*; Barnes & Noble Inc., New York, 1967, p. 115

[36]Sinclair, Upton; *The Jungle*; Robert Bentley, Inc., Boston, 1971

[37]Wells, H. G.; *A Modern Utopia*; University of Nebraska Press, Lincoln, 1967, p. 286

[38]*The Vegetarian Way; op. cit.*, p. 68

[39]Besant, Annie; *Vegetarianism in the Light of Theosophy*; The Theosophical Publishing House, Madras, 1919

[40]Weintraub, Stanley, ed.; *Shaw: An Autobiography*; Vol. 1, Weybright & Talley, New York, 1969, p. 92

[41]*Vegetarianism*; The Vegetarian Society (U.K.) Ltd., Cheshire, England, p. 11

[42]Schweitzer, Albert; *Reverence for Life*; Philosophical Library, New York, 1965, p. 5

[43]Gandhi, M. K.; *The Moral Basis of Vegetarianism*; Navajivan Publishing House Ahmedabad, 1959

[44]Krishnamurti, J.; *The Flight of the Eagle*; Harper & Row, New York, 1971, p. 44

[45]*The Vegetarian Way; op. cit.*, p. 16A

[46]Dinshah, H. Jay; *How to Be a Vegetarian*; The American Vegan Society, Malaga, New Jersey, p. 2

[47]*Liberty Magazine*; Vol. 64, No. 2, March-April, 1969, p. 21

Chapter 2

# COMPARATIVE ANATOMY AND PHYSIOLOGY

Animals do not need to exploit people
to survive. People do not need to exploit
animals to survive.
—Animal Liberation Front

It has been found that the diet of any animal in its natural state agrees both with the animal's anatomical and physiological structure and its general body functions. Man is, of course, a mammal, as are the ape, cow, lion, whale, dog, and horse. In the comparative analysis which follows, we will concern ourselves mainly with the terrestrial vertebrate mammals; i.e., those that possess backbones and live on land. We will then divide these animals into the four main groups: the carnivora (flesh-eaters), the omnivora (those animals that consume both meat and vegetables), the herbivora (grass and leaf eaters), and the frugivora (eaters of fruits, nuts, and grains). In the scientifically documented survey which follows, we will clearly see why man is naturally suited to a fleshless diet.

## The Carnivora

The carnivorous animals include the lion, dog, hyena, wolf, and cat, and they share among themselves many unique characteristics which set them apart from all other members of the animal kingdom.

All carnivorous animals possess a simple digestive system which is only three times the length of the animal's body. It is perfectly suited for the fast digestion and elimination of rapidly decaying organisms.

| THE CARNIVORA | THE OMNIVORA | THE HERBIVORA | THE ANTHROPOID APES | MAN |
|---|---|---|---|---|
| Zonary placenta | Placenta non-deciduate | Placenta non-deciduate | Discoidal placenta | Discoidal placenta |
| Four footed | Four footed | Four footed | Two hands and two feet | Two hands and two feet |
| Have claws | Have hoofs | Have hoofs (cloven) | Flat nails | Flat nails |
| Go on all fours | Go on all fours | Go on all fours | Walks upright | Walks upright |
| Have tails | Have tails | Have tails | Without tails | Without tails |
| Eyes look sideways | Eyes look sideways | Eyes look sideways | Eyes look forward | Eyes look forward |
| Skin without pores | Skin with pores | Skin with pores (save with pachyderms as the elephant) | Millions of pores | Millions of pores |
| Slightly developed incisor teeth | Very well developed incisor teeth | | Well developed incisor teeth | Well developed incisor teeth |
| Pointed molar teeth | Molar teeth in folds | | Blunt molar teeth | Blunt molar teeth |
| *Dental formula 5 to 8.1.6.1.5 to 8 / 5 to 8.1.6.1.5 to 8 | Dental formula 8.1.2 to 3.1.8 / 8.1.2 to 3.1.8 | Dental formula 6.0.0.0.0. / 6.1.6.1.6 | Dental formula 5.1.4.1.5. / 5.1.4.1.5. | Dental formula 5.1.4.1.5 / 5.1.4.1.5 |
| Small salivary glands | Well developed salivary glands | Well developed salivary glands | Well developed salivary glands | Well developed salivary glands |
| Acid reaction of saliva and urine. | Saliva and urine acid | Alkaline reaction, saliva and urine | Alkaline reaction, saliva and urine | Alkaline reaction of saliva and urine |
| Rasping tongue | Smooth tongue | Smooth tongue | Smooth tongue | Smooth tongue |
| Teats on abdomen | Teats on abdomen | Teats on abdomen | Mammary glands on breast | Mammary glands on breast |
| Stomach simple and roundish | Stomach simple and roundish, large cul-de-sac | A stomach in three compartments (in camel and some ruminents four) | Stomach with duodenum (as second stomach) | Stomach with duodenum (as second stomach) |
| Intestinal canal 3 times length of the body | Intestinal canal 10 times length of the body | Length of intestinal canal varies according to species, but is usually 10 times longer than body | Intestinal canal 12 times length of the body | Intestinal canal 12 times length of body |
| Colon smooth | Intestinal canal smooth and convoluted | Intestinal canal smooth and convoluted | Colon convoluted | Colon convoluted |
| Lives on flesh | Lives on flesh, carrion and plants | Lives on grass, herbs and plants | Lives on fruit and nuts | Lives on fruit and nuts |

*The figures in the center represent the number of incisors, upon each side are the canines, followed to the right and left are the molars.

Andrews, A. D.
*Fit Food For Man.*
Chicago, American Natural Hygiene Society Inc.
© 1970, AD Andrews

The bodies of the natural carnivora manufacture acid urine, and their stomachs are rich in hydrochloric acid, which enables them to digest bone and the tough, fibrous tissue found in animal muscle.

Carnivora do not perspire through their skin as do non-meat eaters, but rather sweat through their tongues. One reason for the absence of sweat glands in the carnivora is that by nature they are mainly night hunters, and sleep during the day when it is hot. Therefore they do not need sweat glands and pores to regulate body heat by the evaporation of water from the skin surface. We can observe this characteristic in dogs that have learned to accompany man by day. As they are exposed to greater heat, dogs perspire through their tongues and pant in order to cool off. On the other hand, vegetarian animals such as the cow, horse, camel, zebra and deer spend much of their time in the sun and freely perspire through the skin in order to regulate body temperature.

Perhaps the most significant difference between the natural carnivore and other mammals is found in their dentition or tooth structure. Along with sharp claws all carnivora possess powerful jaws and pointed, elongated canines which are easily capable of spearing and tearing flesh. Meat eating animals also lack the molar teeth which all vegetarians need and use for grinding.

Dr. Alfred S. Romer, Professor Emeritus of Zoology at Harvard University writes:

> The carnivore has to make its kill mainly with its teeth and has to pierce stout hide, cut through tendons and hard bones. On the other hand, flesh is comparatively simple to digest and need not be well chewed. We find, in relation to this, that in the more strictly flesh-eating forms grinding molar teeth have been reduced almost to the vanishing point. A cat, for example, has no chewing power whatever. . . The front part of the dentition is highly developed. The incisors are highly useful in biting and tearing: the canines, or 'dog teeth,' are long and pointed stabbing weapons in all flesh eaters.[1]

## The Omnivora

The omnivorous animals are basically similar in anatomical structure and physiology to the carnivora. The natural omnivora include the raccoon, wild boar, and several varieties of the bear. Man is not included as an omnivore, and we will see why later in this chapter. In the category of natural omnivora are included some of the insect-eating animals whose dental structure enables them to deal with a great variety of foods. Some people tend to classify the pig as an omnivore because it eats carrion along with excrement and other decomposing matter.

As we discovered with the carnivora, we find that the tooth structure of the omnivore is a key to diet. In his discussion regarding the dentition of the omnivorous wild boar, Dr. L. B. Halstead writes in *The Pattern of Vertebrate Evolution:*

> The lower incisors are precumbent for digging, the canines are reverted and are used as weapons, and the cheek teeth have the basic number of four cusps, but the enamel is considerably crinkled to give the multicuspid bunodont condition."[2]

In referring to the dental structure of bears, Dr. Romer writes:

> . . . The bears have veered sharply away from the flesh-eating habits of their ancestors and have redeveloped considerable chewing power. These large forms have, in general, a mixed diet. The last molar tooth had, it would seem, already vanished before the bears drifted back toward a herbivorous type of diet; and teeth, like other structural features generally, when once gone never reappear. But in bears the lack of a full set of back teeth has been made up for by the great elongation of the two molars which are left; the two do the work of three.[4]

In his discussion of the omnivorous raccoons and their mixed diet, Professor Romer continues:

> They have . . . departed far from a carnivorous mode of life. One evidence of this is the fact that the

shearing teeth can no longer shear; they have been modified into chewing teeth like the molars behind them.[5]

## The Herbivora

The herbivorous animals include the cow, camel, elephant, sheep, ox, llama, and deer. These animals generally live on grass, herbs and others plants, much of which is often coarse and bulky in character, and often includes sharp edges. For this reason, the herbivorous animals such as the cow possess twenty-four grinding molar teeth, six on each side of the jaw, with eight cutting teeth on the bottom. Herbivora do not eat merely by opening and shutting their mouths like the cat or the wolf, but in addition use a slight lateral motion used for grinding their food.

They take their water through suction, as opposed to the lapping method which all carnivora (such as the dog) use. The skin of the herbivore contains millions of tiny pores which regulate the body temperature through sweating. Herbivorous animals are also equipped with a complicated series of stomachs and a long, convoluted intestine which is ten times the length of the body. Their saliva contains ptyalin and is alkaline in nature, as is the urine. Since herbivora do not consume rapidly decaying food as do the carnivora, digestion can and does take many hours.

It is also important to note that herbivora do not possess either claws or saber-like teeth, although some grass eaters, such as the rhinoceros, bull, and ram, are equipped with armor or horns used for defending their mates and progeny.

It has also been found recently that flesh food has a decidedly harmful effect on the herbivorous and other vegetarian animals, while no detrimental effects were evidenced in natural carnivora. William S. Collins, M.D. discusses these findings in *Medical Counterpoint*:

> Recent studies, many of them in my laboratory at
> the Maimonides Medical Center, appear to indicate

that the carnivorous animal has almost unlimited capacity to handle saturated fats and cholesterol, whereas the vegetarian and herbivorous animals have a very restricted capacity to handle these food components. It is virtually impossible to produce atherosclerosis in the dog, for example, even when 120 grams (½ lb.) of butter fat are added to his meat ration. This amount of cholesterol is equal to approximately 100 times the amount man normally takes in his food in a typical American diet in a 24-hour period. Yet after two years of such feeding, there were no changes observed in dog arteries. On the other hand, adding only 2 grams of cholesterol daily to a rabbit's chow for two months produces striking fatty changes in his arterial wall.[6]

## The Frugivora

These animals include mainly the anthropoid ape which is said to be our immediate evolutionary ancestor. The diet of the frugivora consists largely of fruits and nuts. They possess a skin with millions of pores, and have blunt molar teeth for grinding and chewing their food.

As is the case of the herbivora, the frugivorous animals produce alkaline urine, and possess alkaline saliva with ptyalin. Their convoluted intestine is twelve times the length of the body, being designed for the slow digestion of vegetables and fruits which are noted for slow decay. The hands of the frugivore contain no claws, and are especially designed for picking and eating the fruits, nuts, and other vegetarian foods it needs.

## Man

Man also has skin with millions of tiny pores, and drinks water by suction, as do the other vegetarian animals. His digestive tract is twelve times the length of his body. His stomach, duodenum, and convoluted intestines are not unlike those of the frugivorous anthropoid ape, but differ from both the grass eaters and the natural flesh-eaters. Man's extremities bear no resemblance to either the hooves of the herbivora or the claws of the carnivora and omnivora, but are perfectly suited for picking and eating fruits, vegetables, and nuts.

As we find in the case of the anthropoid ape, man is equipped with thirty-two teeth including twelve molars and eight premolars which are naturally suited for chewing vegetables and fruits, as well as for cracking nuts. Some people maintain that man's so-called "canine teeth" make him naturally a meat eater. However, many others conclude that the term "canine teeth" is a misnomer, since they obviously bear no real resemblance to the "long and pointed stabbing weapons" found in both the natural carnivore and omnivore. In his article in *Medical Counterpoint,* Dr. Collins writes:

> . . . Man possesses a dental structure designed more like the herbivore than the carnivore. He has sharp cutting incisors (grass cutters), molars which have a flat or nodular surface designed to grind vegetables and fruits, and short dull canines with no capacity for slashing or tearing meats.

Note: Dr. Collins feels that "An important step will be to determine whether man, a vegetarian by design can, by means of any treatment, be given the metabolic capabilities of a carnivore."[8]

Furthermore, it is obvious that our natural instinct is not inclined toward flesh food. Most of us have our meat animals slaughtered by proxy, as we would be sickened if forced to kill these animals ourselves. Instead of eating meat in its natural state as do all carnivora and omnivora, we boil, bake, broil or fry it, and usually disguise it with various gravies and seasonings so that it bears no real resemblance to the original product. In his book *No Animal Food,* R. H. Wheldon discusses this issue frankly and clearly:

> The gorge of a cat, for instance, will rise at the smell of a mouse, or a piece of raw flesh, but not at the aroma of fruit. If a man can take delight in pouncing upon a bird, tear its still living body apart with his teeth, sucking the warm blood, one might infer that Nature had provided him with carnivorous instinct, but the very thought of doing such a thing makes him shudder.

On the other hand, a bunch of luscious grapes makes his mouth water, and even in the absence of hunger he will eat fruit to gratify taste.[9]

As we have seen in the previous analysis, we can conclude that man is naturally neither a carnivore, omnivore, or herbivore. Instead, he is anatomically, physiologically and instinctively suited to a diet of fruits, vegetables, nuts, and grains. A person who adheres to this type of diet is termed a pure vegetarian or "vegan."

Others maintain that from a standpoint of necessity, man is also inclined toward a diet which includes eggs, milk, and other dairy products. Those who consume a vegetable, egg, and dairy food diet are termed "lacto-ovo-vegetarians." A detailed section discussing how one can adjust to a healthful vegetarian diet is included later in the book.

### References

[1]Romer, A. S.; *The Vertebrate Story*; University of Chicago Press, Chicago, 1959, p. 239
[2]Halstead, L. B.; *The Pattern of Vertebrate Evolution*; W. H. Freeman & Co., San Francisco, 1968, p. 161
[3]Romer; *op. cit.*, p. 239
[4]*Ibid.*, p. 250
[5]*Ibid.*, p. 249
[6]Collins, W. S.; "Atherosclerotic Disease: an Anthropologic Theory;" *Medical Counterpoint*; December 1969, pp. 54-5
[7]*Ibid.*, p. 54
[8]*Ibid.*, p. 57
[9]Wheldon, R. H.; *No Animal Food*; Health Culture Co., New York, p. 50


### Other References

Francis, Carl C. and Farrell, G. L.; *Integrated Anatomy and Physiology*; The C. V. Mosby Company, St. Louis, 1957
Hodson, Geoffrey; *Radiant Health from a Meat Free Dietary*; The New Zealand Vegetarian Society, Inc., Auckland
Rudd, Geoffrey L.; *Why Kill for Food?*; The Vegetarian Society, Cheshire, England, 1956

Chapter 3

# VITALITY, HEALTH AND STRENGTH THROUGH A VEGETARIAN DIET

Defile not your body . . . for the body
is the temple of the spirit. . . .
—The Essene Gospel of Peace

As we have just seen in the preceding chapter, meat does not constitute a natural diet for man. However, one cannot deny that man has been able to survive on a diet containing meat for thousands of years.

A gasoline engine can operate on kerosene, but it will clog frequently, wear out sooner, and break down faster than if it were run on gasoline. The human body is not a gasoline engine, but an intricate and wonderful mechanism which is to serve us during our lifetime. It is the vehicle of expression to others; it carries out our daily tasks — it has been called "the horse on which we ride." Without a physical body we would exist in a vacuum. This body is the only one we have in this life. It therefore stands to reason that, like the gasoline engine, it should be given the food which it was built to consume: a natural diet of fruits, grains, nuts, and vegetables. A well-selected vegetarian diet is in harmony with the laws of nature, and will help to assure a healthy, vital, and strong body which serves as the temple for our thoughts, feelings, and spiritual essence.

In this chapter we will study some of the advantages of a vegetarian diet and its proven superiority over meat in regard to nutrition, health, strength, endurance and hygiene.

## Part 1 — *Nutritional Reasons*

There are absolutely no grounds to the assertion that civilized man needs meat in order to enjoy vibrant health and an active, long, and productive life. Frederick J. Stare, M.D., Chairman of the Department of Nutrition at Harvard University, has testified to the value of a non-meat diet:

> There is nothing nutritionally wrong with vegetarian diets: they provide a variety of fruits and vegetables plus frequent use of legumes, particularly soybean products and nuts. Most vegetarians consume generous quantities of milk and eggs. Good vegetarian diets are very healthful.[1]

In the following pages we will take into account the findings of several studies which have analyzed in depth and in detail the nutritional value of a vegetarian diet in a variety of settings and circumstances.

### Rural Studies

Some of this research has taken place in developing regions of the world, and has attempted to evaluate the diets and nutritional level of selected groups of people living in rural areas of these countries.

One of these research teams visited Mexico, and published the following findings in *The American Journal of Public Health*:

> Studies of the nutritional status of several population groups on the high plateau of central Mexico have demonstrated that the common dietary pattern is fundamentally sound. This pattern is based on a liberal consumption of tortillas, beans, and chili peppers, supplemented to a greater or less extent with foods obtained locally. However, the caloric intake is low, little animal protein is consumed.[2]

A more recent study was undertaken in a remote Andean village by a group of medical researchers from Harvard University and the University of Quito in Ecuador. It was

found that many of the four hundred townspeople over
the age of fifteen live to extraordinarily old ages. "The
oldest resident was a 121 year old man. There were several
over 100 years old and 38 over the age of 75. Of these 38,
electrocardiogram studies were done on the 20 oldest, and
only two showed any evidence of heart disease."[3] The
article, which appeared in the *New York Times,* goes on
to say that Dr. Campbell Moses, medical director of the
American Heart Association, called the findings "extra-
ordinary" and said that such electrocardiogram studies of
a similarly elderly population in the United States "would
show 95 per cent with cardiovascular disease." The diet
of these people was found to be basically pure vegetarian,
and included only 153 grams of animal fat—only a third
as much animal fat as consumed by the average adult
American male each day.[4]

In 1939 Major-General Sir Robert McCarrison, once
physician to the King of Great Britain, lived and worked
with the Hunzas of Kashmir. Known throughout the world
for their longevity and freedom from disease, their diet
consists mainly of whole grains, fresh fruits and vegetables,
and goat milk. They occasionally consume goat meat on
feast days, which are rare. Dr. McCarrison wrote:

> I never saw a case of asthenic dyspepsia, of gastric
> or duodenal ulcer, of appendicitis, or mucus colitis
> or cancer. . . Among these people the abdomen over-
> sensitive to nerve impressions, to fatigue, anxiety,
> or cold was unknown.[5]

Dr. McCarrison's findings correlate with those of the
Andean research team: a balanced vegetarian diet means
sound nutrition, longer life and better overall health.


## Wartime Experience

Research was also undertaken in more economically ad-
vanced areas during times of national crisis. One such
study took place in Denmark during the World War I

Allied Blockade which cut off all imports to that country. The government, realizing the possibility of acute food shortages, sought the aid of Denmark's vegetarian society, and appointed Dr. Mikkel Hindhede to direct its rationing program.

Dr. Hindhede later discussed his project in the *Journal of the American Medical Association*:

> Our principal foods were bran bread, barley porridge, potatoes, greens, milk, and some butter . . . the people of the cities and towns got little or no pork. Beef was so costly that only the rich could afford to buy it in sufficient amount. It is evident, therefore, that most of the population was living on a milk and vegetable diet.[6]

The results of this program indicate that the Danish people survived the war with improved health and lowered mortality rates. In the very first year of rationing, the mortality figures fell 17 per cent. In the year 1917-1918, 6,300 fewer people died in Denmark than had died in 1913, which was the previous year in which the mortality rate was lowest.[7]

The *Journal of the American Dietetic Association* reports similar results from rationing in Norway during the Second World War:

> Norway had a similar experience during the war years of 1940-1945 when it became necessary to make drastic cuts in the consumption of popular animal foods and increase the use of fish, cereals, potatoes, and vegetables. Strom and Jensen (in "Mortality from Circulatory Diseases in Norway, 1940-1945") reported the favorable effect of this restriction on the mortality rate from circulatory diseases, as well as the prompt return to prewar levels when the nation returned to its prewar diet at the end of hostilities.[8]

Other scientific research dealing with the growth rates of children found that vegetarian children have equal growth rates as compared with those of children who consume a mixed meat and vegetable diet.[9]

Significant results from another nutritional study, undertaken by Mervyn G. Hardinge, M.D. of the College of Medical Evangelists, Loma Linda, California, and Fredrick J. Stare, M.D., of Harvard University, were published in *The Journal of Clinical Nutrition*.

In their study of 200 vegetarians and nonvegetarians these scientists observed only slight differences in physical measurements, blood pressures, and protein, albumin, and globulin levels. The investigation included adolescents, pregnant women, and adults between 45 and 70 years of age. Each group was divided into (1) lacto-ovo-vegetarians (individuals who refrain from flesh foods but who consume animal products such as milk and eggs); (2) pure vegetarians; and (3) nonvegetarians. Nutrient and caloric intakes were about the same for all groups.

Although laboratory and physical findings were similar in all groups, the pure vegetarians were found to weigh 20 pounds less than the others.[10] The lacto-ovo-vegetarians and the nonvegetarians averaged 12 to 15 pounds above the ideal weight.[11]

Weight gains and losses of pregnant women and average birth weights of infants were similar in vegetarians and nonvegetarians. No evidence indicated that a vegetarian diet is insufficient for expectant mothers, nor did such a diet affect the growth rates of the vegetarian adolescents who participated in the study. The report also found that "There appears to be a tendency for the pure vegetarians to have mean corpuscular volumes somewhat higher than the lacto-ovo-vegetarians and nonvegetarians."[12]

## Part 2 — Health Reasons

In recent years new medical evidence has come to light which has linked a meat diet with several illnesses, specifically gout, heart disease, and other lesser ailments which affect millions of people yearly.

## Gout

The exact causes of this painful disease are unknown, and much research needs to be done if gout is to be eliminated. "Gout is a disturbance in metabolism. The metabolic abnormality results in an unusual use of certain foods (purines) so that the end product of purine metabolism (uric acid) is present in the blood in increased amounts."[13] Purines are found in most kinds of meat, especially the red meat from hogs and cattle. This fact establishes a definite relationship between gout and meat eating.

The medical text *Arthritis and Allied Conditions* instructs patients suffering from gout to avoid liver, sweetbreads, brains, and kidneys, and to omit all meat extractives, broth soups, and gravies. Other types of meat are not completely prohibited, but their consumption is drastically cut to four ounces per week.[14]

## Heart Disease

A nonmeat diet has also been found to be much more healthful than one of meat in the light of heart disease. Supporting testimony was published in the June 3, 1961 issue of the *Journal of the American Medical Association* which says that, ". . . a vegetarian diet can prevent 90 per cent of our thrombo-embolic disease and 97 per cent of our coronary occlusions."[15]

High levels of cholesterol in the blood have been linked to increased chances of developing heart disease. We again mention the study conducted by Drs. Hardinge and Stare, where it was found that plant protein produces lower levels of cholesterol in the body than animal protein:

> The pure vegetarians had significantly lower serum cholesterol than either their lacto-ovo-vegetarian or nonvegetarian counterparts.[16]

Another study which linked atherosclerosis with meat eating was reported by William S. Collens, M.D., a Consultant in Medicine at the Maimonides Medical Center in New York, and retired Clinical Professor of Medicine at the Downstate Medical Center in Brooklyn. In an article appearing in the December, 1969 issue of *Medical Counterpoint,* Dr. Collens writes:

> American men killed in the Korean War showed, even at the age of 22, striking signs of arteriosclerotic disease in their hearts as compared with Korean soldiers who were free of this damage to their blood vessels. The Americans were well fed with plenty of milk, butter, eggs, and meat. The Koreans were basically vegetarians.[17]

Other scientific researchers have explored the effect of a vegetarian diet on blood circulation in humans. Some of the most interesting findings were discovered by Dr. Oxfred Muller, the inventor of the capillary microscope.

> The influence of a vegetable diet presents itself in this way: The capillaries stretch out and their convolutions become straightened out. We thus can see that this form of nourishment causes a certain unburdening of the peripheral section of the blood vessels while the purely meat diet seems to represent a heavy burden.[18]

## Other Benefits

Some of the other health benefits derived from a vegetarian diet can include relief from stomach disorders, improved sleep, increased sensitivity and greater intuitive faculties, reduced body odor, and a lighter, cleaner feeling. Although many vegetarians feel that a meatless diet has been conducive to these benefits, scientific evidence concerning these allegations is lacking at the present time. However, *The New York Times* reported the findings of Dr. Andrew T. Weil, a former physician at Harvard University, who discovered that a vegetarian diet can do much to eliminate recurring colds and allergies.[19]

### Part 3 — Endurance and Strength

Vegetarians are as strong as meat eaters, and in many cases enjoy greater endurance and stamina than those who consume flesh. The results of two important university studies illustrate these facts.

In a series of carefully controlled experiments at Yale University in 1906-07, Dr. Irving Fisher encountered surprising evidence which revealed that vegetarians have nearly twice the stamina of meat eaters. Forty-nine Yale athletes, instructors, doctors and nurses participated in the study, and were divided into three groups: meat eating athletes, vegetarian athletes, and vegetarians involved in sedentary work. Dr. Fisher's findings were published as "The Effects of Diet on Endurance" (Yale Univ. Publications, 1907) and in his book *How to Live*:

> The comparison for arm holding (holding the arms extended) shows a great superiority on the side of the flesh-abstainers. Only 2 of the 15 flesh-eaters taking this test succeeded in holding their arms out over a quarter of an hour, whereas 22 of the 32 abstainers surpassed that limit. None of the flesh-eaters reached half an hour, but 15 of the 32 abstainers exceeded that limit. Of these 9 exceeded an hour, 4 exceeded 2 hours, and 1 exceeded 3 hours.
>
> In respect to deep knee bending, if we use the number 325 for reference, we find that, of the 9 flesh-eaters taking this test only 3 surpassed this figure, while of the 21 abstainers, 17 surpassed it. Only 1 of the 9 flesh-eaters reached 1,000 as against 6 of the 21 abstainers. None of the former surpassed 2,000 as against 2 of the latter.[20]

At about the same time, another study of 42 vegetarians and 25 meat-eating students was carried out by Dr. J. Ioteyko and V. Kipiani at Brussels University. The results were first published as *Inquête Scientifique sur les Végétariens de Bruxelles* in 1907, and proved comparable to those of Dr. Fisher. In the endurance tests, the vegetarians were able to perform two to three times longer than the meat eaters before complete exhaustion, and took only one fifth the time to recover from fatigue after each test than their meat-eating counterparts.[21]

Although the facts presented by these two studies appeared to many as barely short of incredible, curiously enough not one scientific study has been undertaken to disprove these significant findings.

## The Vegetarian Animals

It is also of value to note that the world's strongest, most enduring, and longest lived animals are all vegetarian. We all know of the strength of the elephant, the ox, and the gorilla; the endurance of the camel and horse, and the long life of the tortoise. The bird with the longest life span is the parrot, which lives completely on fruits and seeds.

### Part 4 — Vegetarianism and Athletics

A vegetarian diet has also proven to ensure good health and endurance to individuals under enormous physical and emotional stress: the athlete, Sir Adolphe Abrams, honorary medical officer to the International Athletic Board and the British Athletic Team, wrote that ". . . a vegetarian diet has an adequate caloric value, contains first class animal protein, vitamins and other essentials well balanced in all respects."[22]

Many athletic records in swimming, cross-country running, wrestling, weight lifting, and more than 100 in bicycle racing have been held by vegetarians. Most of these records were set by athletes in Great Britain, where a non-meat diet is more widely accepted than in America.

## Cycling

At one time the Vegetarian Cycling and Athletic Club of Great Britain held as many as 40 per cent of the National Road Records.[23] In a series of fifteen national cycling events held in Great Britain in 1963, vegetarian cyclist Ronald Murgatroid won all fifteen events. Five years later he won the "Best All-Around Veterans Championship" with an average speed for 25 miles, 50 miles, 100 miles, and 12 hours of 22.98 miles per hour.[24] Other vegetarian cyclists have won races which took place throughout the British Isles and Europe, and although they constitute a relatively small percentage of contestants, the vegetarians have consistently made up a higher percentage of winners than their meat eating counterparts.

## Swimming

Perhaps the best known vegetarian athlete is Murray Rose, the swimming champion who became the youngest triple gold medal winner in the Olympic Games by winning the 400 and 1500-meter freestyle and 1500-meter marathon events at the 1956 Olympic Games in Melbourne, Australia. Four years later, at the 1960 Olympic Games in Rome, he became the first man in history to retain his 400-meter title. In later years he broke earlier records for the 400-meter and 1500-meter freestyle events, leaving his mark as one of the greatest swimmers of all time.[25]

Other swimming achievements were made by Bill Pickering, a British vegetarian who won fame in 1956 for swimming the English Channel faster than anyone in history. "Not content with conquering the English Channel . . . in record time, [48 year old] Bill has now set up another record in crossing the Bristol Channel . . . in the magnificent time of 6 hours 20 minutes. It was the first crossing by any swimmer for forty years . . ."[26]

## Weight Lifting

In support of the claim that a vegetarian diet is conducive to strength as well as good health, included herewith is a paragraph describing the feats of Mr. Alexander Macpherson Anderson, known professionally as "The

Mighty Young Apollo." This professional strong man has secured many world and Australian weight lifting records in all class divisions.

> Apollo has pulled the greatest tonnage by his teeth of anyone in the world. He twice drew up a slight incline for a distance of 100 yards a fully loaded electric tram weighing approximately 22½ tons. On various occasions he has also pulled by the teeth four "Sun" newspaper delivery trucks, five passenger automobiles hitched together, and a double decker bus.
> Apollo changed to a vegetarian diet early in 1951. He has found no diminution of his strength since the change. . .[27]

## Effects of a Vegetarian Diet on Meat Eating Athletes

It has also been found that a meatless diet can improve the records of nonvegetarian athletes:

> "Johnny Weismuller . . . world swimming champion, was invited to the dedication of a new swimming pool at the Battle Creek Sanitorium. Weismuller had made 56 world records, but for five years had made no new ones. After several weeks on a well-selected vegetarian diet, he was able to hang up six more world records in the swimming pool."[28]

An October 1970 article in *Sports Illustrated* about former Oakland Raiders linebacker Chip Oliver (called by his manager "one of the finest young prospects in football,")[29] testified to the success of a vegetarian diet:

> In fact, he played better after becoming a vegetarian, winning a starting berth with five games to go.[30]

A large volume of additional information documents many other athletic achievements by vegetarians in cross-country running, wrestling, and boxing, as well as more successes in swimming, cycling, and feats of strength. However, these sources are generally difficult to come by because they are not in general demand. Some can be found nevertheless in vegetarian societies, some health food stores, and some libraries as well.

### References

[1]*Ladies' Home Journal*; Vol. LXXXVII, No. 10, October 1971, p. 72

[2]*American Journal of Public Health*; No. 38, 1948, p. 1126

[3]*The New York Times*; April 22, 1971, p. 43

[4]*Ibid.*

[5]Marine, Gene and Van Allen, Judith; *Food Pollution: The Violation of Our Inner Ecology*; Holt, Rinehart and Winston, New York, 1972, p. 19

[6]Hindhede, M.; "The Effect of Food Restriction During War on Mortality in Copenhagen;" *Journal of the American Medical Association*; Vol. 74, No. 6, February 7, 1920, p. 381

[7]*Ibid.*

[8]*Journal of the American Dietetic Association*; *op. cit.*, p. 548

[9]Von Haller, Albert; *The Vitamin Hunters*; The Chilton Co., Philadelphia, 1962, p. 140

[10]*The Journal of Clinical Nutrition*; Vol. 2, No. 2, March-April, 1954, pp. 74-5, 77

[11]*The Journal of the American Dietetic Association*; *op. cit.*, p. 553

[12]*The Journal of Clinical Nutrition*; *op. cit.*, pp. 80-81

[13]*The Encyclopedia Americana*; Vol. 13, The Americana Corp., New York, 1957, p. 87

[14]Hollander, J. L., ed.; *Arthritis and Allied Conditions*; Lea & Febiger, Philadelphia, 1966, p. 937

[15]"Diet and Stress in Vascular Disease;" *Journal of the American Medical Association*; Vol. 176, No. 9, June 3, 1961, p. 806

[16]"Non-Flesh Dietaries;" *The Journal of the American Dietetic Association*; *op. cit.*, p. 554

[17]Collens, W. S.; "Atherosclerotic Disease: An Anthropologic Theory;" *Medical Counterpoint*; December 1969, p. 55

[18]Von Haller; *op. cit.*, p. 246

[19]"Meat Eating 230-Pound Doctor is Now 175-Pound Vegetarian;" *The New York Times*; August 12, 1971, p. 38

[20]Fisher, Irving and Fisk, Eugene L.; *How to Live*; Funk & Wagnalls Co., New York, 1925, pp. 252-3

[21]Buttner, J. L.; *A Fleshless Diet: Vegetarianism as a Rational Dietary*; Frederick A. Stokes Co., New York, 1910, pp. 131-2

[22]*Practitioner*; No. 187, 1962, p. 183

[23]Rudd, Geoffrey; *Why Kill for Food?*; The Vegetarian Society, Cheshire, England, 1956, p. 104

[24]*The British Vegetarian*; Vol. 10, No. 5, Sept.-Oct. 1968, p. 413

[25]*Current Biography 1962*; The H. W. Wilson Co., New York, 1963, pp. 365-6

[26]*The British Vegetarian*; Vol. 11, No. 5, Sept.-Oct. 1969, p. 469

[27]Hodson, Geoffrey; *Vegetarian Foods—Their Nutrient Properties*; *op. cit.*, p. 21

[28]Parrett, Owen, M.D.; *Why I Don't Eat Meat*; Modern Publications, St. Catherines, Ontario, 1966, p. 8

[29]*Sports Illustrated*; Vol. 33, No. 15, October 12, 1970, p. 50

[30]*Ibid.*, p. 51

Chapter 4

# HYGIENE

The numerous examples cited in the preceding pages cast strong doubts as to the supposed superiority of a meat diet over vegetarian fare, particularly in regard to nutrition, health, and strength. In the following several sections of this chapter, we will see why flesh is in reality an inferior and even dangerous food to ingest into the human body.

From a viewpoint of hygiene, there are five basic factors to consider which attest to the impurity and danger of a meat diet for humans. These factors include the rapid decomposition of meat, impurities within the animal's body, the phenomenon of "pain poisoning," the residues of pesticides, and the danger of chemical additives found in meat.

## *Rapid Decomposition*

The meat of a healthy live animal is said to be fairly sterile. The number of bacteria found in meat when it is ready to eat is a kind of post-mortem history of the carcass' trip from the slaughtering line to the dinner table. It is the nature of animal flesh to putrefy in a very short time, as meat is composed of rapidly decaying cell nuclei. By the time the animal is slaughtered, the meat placed in cold storage, "aged," transported to various warehouses, butchershops, and supermarkets, cut up for packaging, exposed on store displays, purchased, brought home, stored, prepared, and finally served, literally billions of pathogenic organisms have been given time to generate a highly toxic poison. Many times this decomposition cannot be detected by our sense of smell, and often these bacteria cannot be cooked out, since meat is an excellent insulator. By the time the piece of meat becomes even remotely sterilized at very high and prolonged temperatures, it is usually well overdone.

This problem of putrefying meat was brought into focus in the February, 1972 issue of *Consumer Reports*. After having studied samples from 32 brands of frankfurters purchased from supermarkets throughout the United States, the researchers made the following observations:

> Food experts generally agree that putrefaction has set in when a frankfurter's total bacteria count has reached 10 million per gram. With that as a yardstick, more than 40 per cent of the samples we analyzed had begun to spoil. One sample tested out at 140 million bacteria per gram.[1]

Regarding the process of aging, page 35 of the *Meat Packing Plant Operation Manual* reads:

> (Aging consists of) . . . a gradual and partial transformation of the more complex constituents of meat into simpler compounds. These changes consisted chiefly of increases in acidity, in proteose, noncoagulable amino, and ammoniacal nitrogen and in soluble inorganic phosphorus, decreases in coagulable nitrogen and soluble organic phosphorus.[2]

One of the world's foremost experts in the science of yoga, Swami Vishnudevananda, expressed his understanding of aging in simpler terms:

> When alive, animal muscle tissue is tender, but after death, stiffening from the coagulation of the muscular tissues sets in. The meat toughens and never becomes tender again until it putrefies. This is why meat is kept for some time to "ripen," or in other words, to decay.[3]

### Bodily Poisons

In addition to the natural decomposition of cells, the body of a live animal, like that of a human being, is constantly purifying itself of poisons which are found in the body. During life, body tissues are washed by a pure stream of blood, which gathers up the waste substances and carries them to the liver, kidneys and skin for elimination. When the heart ceases to beat, this cleansing process ceases as well. These body poisons, along with the already decomposing cells after death, poison the entire carcass. *The Encyclopaedia Britannica* discusses the subject in this way:

> Toxic wastes, including uric acid, are present in the blood and tissue, as also are dead and virulent bacteria, not only from the putrefactory process, but from animal diseases, such as hoof and mouth disease, contagious abortion, swine fever, malignant tumors, etc. Similarly, meat contains vaccines injected into the animals against prevalent diseases.
>
> Proteins obtained from nuts, pulses, grains and dairy produce is said to be relatively pure as compared with beef with a 56% impure water content.[4]

### Pain Poisoning

In humans it is generally accepted that fear, rage, and pain produce chemical changes within the body. Nobel Prize winning surgeon and biologist, Dr. Alexis Carrel, discussed this matter in his book, *Man The Unknown*:

> Emotions . . . determine the dilatation or the contraction of the small arteries, through the vasomotor nerves. . . . The affective states act on all glands by increasing or decreasing their circulation. They stimulate or stop the secretions, or modify their chemical constitution.[5]

When humans become very angry, fearful or are shocked, we find that these psychological traumas can produce physical illness, as certain fluids poison the system in times of extreme stress. Human beings are not alone in this regard; other members of the animal kingdom

are affected by the same causes. In the textbook
*Meat Through the Microscope* we find:

> It has been shown that the secretion from the adrenal
> medulla can influence the rate of metabolism. The
> erection of hairs, — on a dog, for example, — the
> ruffling of feathers, the constriction of the capillaries,
> and the increase of sugar in the blood, are well known
> phenomena when warm blooded animals are exposed
> to the cold. Adrenaline is responsible for these re-
> sults. Anger also increases the activity of the gland;
> thus rage really exercises the suprarenal capsule. . .[6]

Just as our bodies are made ill during times of intense
rage or pain, so do those of livestock animals. Just before
and during the agony of being slaughtered, large quantities of adrenalin are forced through the entire body, thus
pain-poisoning the entire carcass. Even the meat industry
acknowledges that pre-slaughter psychological stress produces physical changes in the carcass. At the present time
there is concern about the fact that stress causes meat to
actually change color,[7] and in a recent interview, a spokes-
man from the American Meat Institute conceded that
there are many more implications to pain-poisoning which
are yet to be understood.[8]

## The Danger of Pesticides in Meat

One must also take into account the problem of the high
pesticide content of meat. It is well known that all livestock consume their nutriment from the plant kingdom,
which is at a low level of what is known as the "food
chain." When we eat the animals that feed on plants, we
find ourselves eating at a higher level of the food chain.
Scientific evidence has shown us that the higher up on the
food chain one goes for food, the more concentrated the
levels of persistent pesticides, such as the chemical DDT.
Rachel Carson expands on this point in *Silent Spring*:

> One of the most sinister features of DDT and re-
> lated chemicals is the way they are passed on from
> one organism to another through all the links of the

food chains. . . Through such a process of transfer, what started out as a very small amount of DDT may end up as a heavy concentration.[9]

Evidence presented at the International Symposium on Food Protection held at Iowa State University in 1962 showed that most of the DDT found in humans comes from meat and related products. During the same convention, there was presented results of another study which measured the levels of DDT in the fat of human beings. The results disclosed that the average concentration of DDT in the general population of the United States was 4.9 parts per million, while the average concentration found in those who abstain from meat was only 2.3 parts per million per person — less than half.[10]

This process of accumulation results from the fact that organochlorine pesticides like DDT and Dieldrin are retained in animal and fish fat and are difficult to break down. Thus, as big fish eat smaller fish, or as cows eat grass (or feed), whatever pesticides they eat are largely retained and passed on. So if man is eating at the "top" of such food chains, he becomes the final consumer and thus the recipient of the highest concentration of pesticide residues.[11]

## Chemical Additives in Meat

The pesticide threat can appear to be minor when one considers the enormous amounts of chemicals which are found in animal flesh. These chemicals are added to meat in order to preserve it, improve the color, texture, taste and nutritional value, and are added to the feed of the animal so that it may gain weight faster.

The Ralph Nader research group, the Center for Study of Responsive Law (Nader's Raiders) presented the following testimony concerning additives in meat, which was based on exhaustive investigation of the processing and marketing of meat products:

The problem is that residues of many invisible chemicals remain in the meat, endangering the final

consumer, man. Some, like nitrate and nitrate preservatives, can be poisonous under certain conditions.[12]

Related charges were published in the July 18, 1971
edition of *The New York Times*:

> But far greater potential danger to the consumer's
> health are the hidden contaminants: bacteria-like
> salmonella and residues from the use of pesticides,
> nitrates, hormones, antibiotics and other chem-
> icals. . .[13]

However the greatest concern stems from the use of a
particular hormone known as diethylstilbestrol (DES),
which when added to feed cause cattle and sheep to grow
very rapidly, adding as much as 500 pounds to the animal's
weight in a few months' time. The November 8, 1971
issue of *Newsweek* reports:

> There is mounting evidence for a link between
> DES and cancer. Mice, rats, rabbits, and guinea
> pigs in several different university experiments have
> been fed diets with as little as 6.25 parts per million
> of the artificial hormone for every one billion parts
> of ordinary food—and shown a significantly higher
> rate of cancer than control animals.[14]

The same report continues:

> Some 75 per cent of the 34 million beef cattle and
> 16 million sheep that wind up on American dinner ta-
> bles each year have been fattened on feedlots where
> DES has been sprinkled on their fodder.[15]

At this writing, several legal battles are concerned with
the banning of DES in animal feed. However the *National Health Federation Bulletin* reports that two even
more powerful growth stimulants have been developed and
are being used on cattle and sheep.

The first of these chemicals is the synthetic hormone
melengestrol acetate, also known as MGA. Although little information is available concerning its effects, MGA
provides a 6% weight gain over DES and requires a much
shorter time for withdrawal before slaughter.

Zeranol can be used up to three times before slaughter, and presently has a withdrawal period of 65 days. However, it has been found to be effective for up to 125 days after being implanted in the ears of cattle and lambs.[16]

Aside from these chemicals, a partial listing of meat additives includes antibiotics fed or injected into farm animals such as chlortetracycline, arsanilic acid, phenothiazine, phthalysulfacetamide, oxytetracycline, dimetridazole, and ethylenediaminedihydriodide; growth promoters such as progesterone, testosterone propionate, furazolidone, 3-nitro-4-hydroxyphenyl arsenic acid, sodium arsanilate, and tylosin phosphate; and tranquilizers which include promazine, reserpine, and zinc bacitracin.[17] The principal post-mortem additives include the preservatives sodium nitrate, and sodium nitrite, which is a recognized poison.[17a]

## The Need for Inspection

A survey dealing with the healthful benefits of a vegetarian diet would not be complete without a discussion concerning the inspection of meat by federal, state, and local agencies.

It was pointed out earlier that meat decays rapidly by nature. During the interim between the slaughter and the meat purchase by the consumer, much careful inspection is necessary in order to protect the buyer from any impurities which might develop in the meat as well as to guard against any unethical or careless practices on the part of the food handlers.

In addition, we must acknowledge the danger of diseases in the animals. In the text *The Meat Handbook,* we find that "there are over 70 known diseases that animals may have that can be transmitted to man."[18] Some of these diseases include salmonella, distoma, echinococcus, melanosis, tuberculosis, telangiectasis, carotinosis[19]; Q fever, brucellosis, paratyphoid fever, hog cholera, tularemia, vibriosis, glanders, listeriosis, trichinosis, taeniasis, trematodiasis[20]; toxoplasmosis[21]; and leukemia[22]. (Note: This list does not include diseases brought about through the use of additives given to the animals before and/or after death.)

The United States Department of Agriculture Meat Inspection Act of 1906 was passed after the furor which followed publication of *The Jungle* by Upton Sinclair. The provisions of this act apply only to those meat packing establishments which slaughter, render, and prepare meat for interstate shipment and foreign commerce. According to the U.S.D.A. Statistical Reporting Service, approximately 16% of the slaughterhouses in the United States are under Federal inspection, which supply approximately 85% of the meat produced in the United States. In actual numbers, there are 984 slaughterhouses which are Federally inspected while 5172 are not.[23]

Many states have established regulations concerning the inspection of slaughterhouses which are not inspected by the Federal government. During the 1968 Congressional hearings, Mr. Rodney Leonard, Deputy Assistant Secretary of the U.S.D.A. Consumer Marketing Service testified that "There are 42 states with some form of a meat inspection statute—two require only mandatory licensing of packers with no provision for actual inspection of meat; 11 provide for only voluntary programs and 29 have mandatory inspection laws."[24]

## Meat Inspection?

On paper it appears that most of the meat, poultry, and fish that is consumed by the American public is carefully and thoroughly examined by an adequate number of trained, competent inspectors at the federal, state, and local levels.

In practice, however, evidence has shown this not to be the case. In the commentary in which he reviewed the evidence presented at the International Symposium on Food Protection, M. H. Bartram of the United States Food and Drug Administration wrote:

> The presence of parasites in the flesh of meat animals and fish is undoubtedly a problem of considerable magnitude and one that with some exceptions has not received deserved significance and control.[25]

In her book entitled *Poisons in Your Food,* Ruth Winter points out the fallacy of inspected meat:

> Although Federal inspection of interstate meat by the United States Department of Agriculture has been in force since 1906, and although twenty-seven states have mandatory inspection for intrastate meats, the reports of U.S.D.A. inspectors, factory workers, and scientists about some of the meat eaten by unsuspecting Americans today is enough to make a person a vegetarian.[26]

On March 4, 1968, an article published in *The New York Times* reported that a New York City health inspector walked into a Federally inspected Kosher sausage and frankfurter manufacturing firm in February 1968 and found seventy-five violations. These violations included a wide range of findings:

> The worn gears in the meat grinder were rusty and caked with bits of old fat and meat. Paint was scaling off the equipment and falling into the hot dog mixtures. Fresh meat was being stored in rusty tubs.
>
> A sterilizer required in Federal plants to contain 180-degree water for sterilization of knives that are dropped on the floor was full of cold, greasy water. A dead roach floated in the scum of the water surface.
>
> Evidence of rats was everywhere, even where meat was being handled. And there was a Federal inspector on the premises.[27]

In both 1962 and 1967, United States Department of Agriculture inspectors surveyed hundreds of meat packing establishments. According to Minnesota Senator Walter F. Mondale they found the following:

> In virtually every jurisdiction instances of unsanitary meat, unwholesome meat, unsanitary packing

conditions, the introduction of additives such as water
and other fillers, and the misleading labeling requirements were widely found in all jurisdictions to
be beneath the standards of Federal inspection.[28]

A visit by this author to the hog kill floor of one of the
country's most modern slaughterhouses revealed that the
U.S.D.A. have very little time to adequately inspect for
disease the carcasses which pass before them at the rate of
up to eleven hundred per hour. It was also found that if
a cancer or some other disease is discovered, the infected
part of the animal is removed, but the remainder of the
carcass which nurtured that particular malignancy or
disease is passed on for human consumption.

In comparison with state and local inspection, the United States Department of Agriculture is supposed to provide superior meat inspection, and on paper, state and
local inspection is required to be equal to the Federal
levels. After reading the findings published in *Consumer
Reports,* one wonders what state and local meat inspection
must be like:

> We found that one-eighth of the Federally inspect-
> ed sausage and more than one-fifth of the other (non-
> Federally inspected) sausage contained insect frag-
> ments, larvae, rodent hairs, and other kinds of filth. . .
> To put it bluntly, Federal inspection is evidently fail-
> ing to do its job. These evidences of filth, high
> bacteria counts and short weighing, remember,
> emerge from a selection of Federally inspected sausage
> bought in five widely separated states. (New York,
> Pennsylvania, Illinois, New Mexico and California.)
> Furthermore, quality was so low that something
> should be done to inspire better manufacturing and
> distribution practices.[29]

At the time of this writing, legislation is being enacted
which will eventually turn meat inspection entirely over to
the states, with U.S.D.A. "supervision."[30]

Many slaughterhouses consent to giving tours of their
facilities to the public. (In some there are age restrictions,
and others do not permit women to witness the slaughtering operations.) If anyone wishes to verify some of the

facts for himself, individual or group tours can usually be arranged by contacting the public relations department of a meat packing plant.

## References

[1] *Consumer Reports*; February 1972, p. 76

[2] Paddock, L. S. and Ramsbottom, J. M.; "The Aging and Tendering of Meats;" *Meat Packing Plant Operation Manual*; The American Meat Institute, Chicago, 1955, p. 35

[3] Swami Vishnudevananda; *The Complete Illustrated Book of Yoga*; Bell Publishing Co. Inc., New York, 1960, p. 207

[4] *The Encyclopaedia Britannica*; Vol. 22, Encyclopaedia Britannica Inc., Chicago, 1967, p. 935

[5] Carrel, Alexis; *Man The Unknown*; Harper and Brothers, New York, 1935, p. 144

[6] Moulton, C. R.; *Meat Through the Microscope*; University of Chicago, Chicago, 1953, p. 510

[7] American Meat Institute Center for Continuing Education; *The Science of Meat and Meat Products*; W. H. Freeman & Co., San Francisco, 1960, p. 263

[8] Interview with D. D. MacKinsey, American Meat Institute, Chicago, November 9, 1971

[9] Carson, Rachel; *Silent Spring*; Houghton Mifflin Co., Boston, 1962, pp. 22-3

[10] Ayres, J. C. et al.; *Chemical and Biological Hazards in Food*; Iowa State University Press, Ames, Iowa, 1962, p. 144

[11] Lappé, Frances Moore; *Diet for a Small Planet*; Ballantine Books, New York, 1971, p. 19

[12] *Time Magazine*; August 2, 1971, p. 46

[13] *The New York Times*; July 18, 1971, p. 45

[14] *Newsweek*; November 8, 1971, p. 85

[15] *Ibid.*, p. 85

[16] *National Health Federation Bulletin*; October 1971, p. 24

[17] Yeary, Roger A.; *Medicated Feed Additives*; University of California Agricultural Extension Service, Berkeley, 1966, pp. 7-18

[17a] *Consumer Reports*; February 1972, p. 77

[18] Levy, Albert; *The Meat Handbook*; The Avi Publishing Co., Inc., Westport, Conn., 1967, p. 13

[19] Ziegler, P. Thomas; *The Meat We Eat*; The Interstate Publishers and Printers, Inc., Danville, Ill., 1966, p. 26

[20] Campbell, J. R. and Leslie, J. F.; *The Science of Animals that Serve Mankind*; McGraw Hill Book Co., New York, 1969, pp. 476, 478, 485-9, 492, 494-5

[21] *Newsweek*; November 29, 1971, pp. 67-8

[22] *Animal Diseases*; United States Department of Agriculture, Washington, 1956, p. 469

[23] *Livestock Slaughter 1971*; Statistical Reporting Service, U.S.D.A., Washington, D.C., April 1972, p. 35

[24]Winter, Ruth; *Poisons in Your Food*; Crown Publishers Inc., New York, 1969, p. 80

[25]Ayres, J. C. *et al.*; *op. cit.*, pp. 270-1

[26]Winter; *op. cit.*, p. 80

[27]*The New York Times*; March 4, 1968, p. 74

[28]Winter; *op. cit.*, p. 82

[29]*Consumer Reports*; August 1968, pp. 410, 412

[30]*The New York Times*; July 18, 1971, p. 45

## Chapter 5

# THE WORLD FOOD SHORTAGE, ECONOMY AND ECOLOGY

.... the billion people in the developed countries
use practically as much cereals as feed to produce
animal protein as the two billion people of the developing countries use directly as food.

—Lyle P. Schertz, U.S.D.A.

Within the past few years, increasing air, water and land
pollution has brought the issue of ecology—man's relationship with his environment—into sharp focus. People
from every part of the world are slowly beginning to
realize that unless we learn to conserve, respect, and protect the natural resources of the earth, every living in-
habitant of this planet will perish from lack of pure water,
clean air, and arable land.

Closely related to ecology is the problem of the world
food deficit: the gap between the people who require food,
and the amount of food that is actually available for consumption. Many observers feel that this food-population
gap will reach catastrophic proportions by the year 2000
and will affect even those living in the well-fed countries
of today.

During the past few years a significant amount of scientific evidence in favor of the non-meat diet has been offered
in the quest for bringing about a practical and humane
solution to these problems. In this chapter we will objec-
tively study the issues, employing data and testimony supplied by experts in the fields of agriculture, economics
and ecology.

## The World Food Shortage

According to recent official estimates of the Food and Agriculture Organization of the United Nations (FAO), between one and one-and-a-half billion of the world's population are either hungry or malnourished, and among them nearly 500 million barely have enough food on which to live at all.[1] In terms of the world food deficit, there is a world-wide shortage of more than eight million tons of food, which will increase to an estimated one hundred million tons by the year 2000.[2]

## Inefficiency of a Meat Diet

Many agricultural experts and economists feel that one of the chief factors which impairs the achievement of an adequate world food supply is the gross inefficiency of an animal diet in giving people an adequate return for land used. All livestock animals originally obtain their nutriment from plants, thus drawing heavily on those sources of vegetable protein which are later to be converted into animal products, such as meat, milk, and eggs.

The need for eliminating the inefficient conversion of plant food into animal products has been stressed by such individuals as the Director General of the FAO, Mr. A. H. Boerma:

> But if we are to bring about a real improvement
> in the diet of the neediest, we must aim at a greater
> intake of vegetable protein.[3]

Such concern is based on the fact that animals do not produce nearly as much edible protein as they take from the plant food on which they live. For example, a steer provides man with only 43 pounds of protein per acre of land per year,[4] while wheat supplies 269 pounds of protein per acre of land per year.[5] By eliminating the meat diet, we are able to make much better use of productive land, thus providing more people with an adequate diet rich in proteins and the other essential food elements needed for good health. Regarding the production of plant and animal protein output, economic analyst Louis H. Bean made the following statement to the Committee on the World Food Crisis in Washington:

> An acre of land producing feed for cattle, hogs, poultry, or milk can provide a moderately active man with his protein requirements for less than 250 days . . . whereas an acre of dry edible beans will take care of his protein needs for over 1100 days, split peas 1785 days, and edible soybeans over 2200 days, a ratio of 10 to 1 in favor of soybeans over beef. The productivity of grains lies between these extremes.[6]

This testimony is further supported by Dr. Aaron M. Altschul, Chief Research Chemist of the Seed Protein Pioneering Research Laboratory of the United States Department of Agriculture. In his book *Proteins: Their Chemistry and Politics,* Dr. Altschul writes:

> . . . soybeans produce 7.1X more available aminoacids per acre than milk and 8.2X more than eggs. In terms of the average pounds of amino acids per acre, the soybean produces close to 17 lb. per acre compared with about 2 for milk and less than one for beef.[7]

### Our Wasted Resources

At the present time, we are misusing billions of acres of valuable crop land which can be utilized much more efficiently by providing food directly to people. In *The United States and World Resources,* we are told that:

> Slightly more than half the entire harvested acreage in the United States is planted to feed crops. If this acreage were to be used for the direct production of food crops rather than for crops which are now converted into animal products, the total production of food measured in calories could be at least four times as great.[8]

In an address presented at the Sixteenth National Institute of Animal Agriculture, the Dean of the College of Agriculture and Home Economics at Ohio State University conceded:

> The supply of human food could be increased about 35 per cent if the world's human population were to consume these animal utilized vegetable calories directly rather than to utilize them for animal production as is now being done.[9]

If we again utilize information supplied by the United States Department of Agriculture, we can find that approximately 91% of the corn, 77% of the soybean meal, 64% of the barley, 88% of the oats, and 99% of the grain sorghum crops used in the United States in 1971 were fed directly to livestock animals.[10] The inefficiency of meat production invariably makes meat and animal products more costly to the consumer, and as valuable plant resources are wasted through animal use, the cost of available plant food for people is also adversely affected. While at best the resulting high food prices pose somewhat of a bother to the well-fed minority, nearly two billion others are confronted with a real obstacle. A 1970 FAO report on agriculture concerns itself with these problems:

> The production of animal products is subject to severe constraints that threaten to accentuate inequalities of food consumption among socio-economic groups.[11]

This problem is further aggravated by the practice of feeding to farm animals high protein fish meal which could be better utilized to feed millions of starving people throughout the world. Although it is not the author's purpose to endorse the eating of fish, it is a fact that the prevailing geographical and social conditions of many people (such as those living in extreme northern or southern latitudes and the undeveloped coastal regions of the world) limit the effective utilization of vegetable protein. Fully one half of the world fish catch of 1968 was fed directly to livestock instead of people;[12] a total of thirty-two million, one hundred fifty thousand metric tons.[13]

## Pollution of Air, Water, and Land

Another serious problem confronting man is that of the effect of a flesh diet on the overall environment. If the subject is considered in the light of scientific research and direct observation, it can be seen that in regard to ecology, a vegetarian diet is far superior to one including meat.

## Pollution and the Slaughterhouse

If one ventures to any of the nearly 7000 meat packing houses in the United States and Canada, he can clearly see why the meat industry is considered to be one of the country's most arrogant polluters of the air, landscape, and water. As any person unfortunate enough to live near a slaughterhouse knows, the meat packing plant belches obnoxious odors into the air up to twenty-four hours per day. Some of the more sophisticated slaughterhouses attempt to lessen the stench by mixing perfumes with the smoke, but this practice does little to eliminate the poisonous substances which are discharged in these smokestack emissions.

Aside from the unappealing sight the slaughterhouse casts on the landscape, the meat packing houses are also discharging billions of gallons of sewage into the nation's waterways. This poses a significant problem, because these wastes contain enormous quantities of fat, nitrates and phosphates[14] which are notorious for the damage they cause to the surrounding lakes, rivers, and streams.

## The Feedlots

Although slaughterhouse pollution is a serious problem, a still graver problem stems from the feedlots where livestock are fattened up before slaughter. There are approximately 206,000 feedlots in the United States, and they range from the size of a small corral holding a dozen animals, to a mammoth operation in which several hundred thousand animals are fed at one time. The liquid and solid wastes from millions of these livestock animals often percolate directly into the soil, or flow into lakes, streams, and rivers, causing tremendous damage. In the words of Harold Bernard, an agricultural expert with the United States Environmental Protection Agency, "[Feedlot] runoffs carry wastes that are ten to several hundred times more concentrated than raw domestic sewage."[15]

In the same article which contains Dr. Bernard's comments, the author comments that:

> When the highly concentrated wastes in a runoff flow into a stream or river, the results can be—and frequently are—catastrophic. The amount of dissolved oxygen in the waterway will be sharply reduced, while levels of ammonia, nitrates, phosphates and bacteria soar.[16]

## Water Conservation

To compound this problem of water pollution, research has shown that meat eaters are consuming more than their fair share of the pure water that is still usable for consumption. When we consider the per capita quantity of water used daily, we must bear in mind certain factors: the water used in irrigating crops, the drinking water for the livestock animals, the water utilized by the slaughterhouse, and the water used in the washing and preparation of the food before we eat it. In *Proteins: Their Chemistry and Politics,* Dr. Altschul compares the water usage and price factor in the pure vegetarian diet, and the "normal" mixed diet consumed by most people in the United States today:

> The all vegetable regimen would require 300 gallons of water per person per day. The mixed animal and vegetable diet requires 2500 gallons. For food

alone, the cost of maintaining a human being is some-
where between 300 and 2500 gallons of water per day.
The cost of water per pound of meat is about 25
times that of the cost for a pound of vegetables.[17]

The following charts deal with protein output, food
supplies, population growth and cost comparisons between foods of plant and animal origin.

### Table 5-1
**RELATIVE COST OF PROTEIN FROM SELECTED
RAW MATERIAL SOURCES: 1965[18]**

1. Soy Flour (food) .. 11¢ per pound
2. Fish Meal (feed) .... 14¢
3. Cottonseed (flour) ........ 17¢
4. Wheat (whole) .................. 30¢
5. Dry Skim Milk ............... 40¢
6. Peanut Meal
       (defatted)       ................... 43¢
7. Bulgur                      ........................ 47¢
8. Wheat (flour)        ............................. 60¢
9. Chicken (dressed) ................................................. $1.50
10. Beef (retail) ............................................................................................ $4.44

### Table 5-2
**NUMBER OF DAYS OF PROTEIN REQUIREMENTS
PRODUCED BY ONE ACRE[19]**

| Selected Food Products: | Days |
|---|---|
| Beef Cattle | 77 |
| Hogs | 129 |
| Poultry | 185 |
| Milk | 236 |
| Corn Flakes | 354 |
| Oat Meal | 395 |
| Rye Flour (whole) | 485 |
| Wheat Flour (white) | 527 |
| Rice (white) | 654 |
| Rice (brown) | 772 |
| Corn Meal | 773 |
| Wheat Flour (whole) | 877 |
| Beans, Dry Edible | 1116 |
| Peas, Split | 1785 |
| Soybeans, Edible | 2224 |

## Table 5-3

**FUTURE POPULATION INDEX NUMBERS AND RELATED RATES OF GROWTH (1965 = 100)[20]**

| YEAR | LESS DEVELOPED REGIONS | | DEVELOPED REGIONS | | WORLD | |
|---|---|---|---|---|---|---|
| | Millions | Index Numbers | Millions | Index Numbers | Millions | Index Numbers |
| 1965 | 2,452 | 100 | 907 | 100 | 3,359 | 100 |
| 1980 | 3,459 | 141 | 1,049 | 116 | 4,508 | 134 |
| 2000 | 5,356 | 218 | 1,274 | 140 | 6,630 | 197 |

Annual % Rates of Increase (Compound)

| | | | |
|---|---|---|---|
| 1965-1980 | 2.3 | 1.0 | 2.0 |
| 1980-2000 | 2.2 | 1.0 | 1.9 |

## Table 5-4

**TOTAL FOOD SUPPLIES AVAILABLE AND NEEDED IN THE WORLD[21]**
(millions of metric tons per year)

| | Available in 1965 | Needed under short-term goal | | Needed under long-term goal | |
|---|---|---|---|---|---|
| | | 1965 | 1980 | 1965 | 2000 |
| Cereals and starchy roots | 722 | 730 | 977 | 682 | 1,348 |
| Pulses | 51 | 63 | 84 | 76 | 148 |
| Fruits and Vegetables | 311 | 343 | 461 | 402 | 789 |
| Animal Foods | 387 | 427 | 573 | 513 | 1,007 |
| Fats and Oils | 27 | 29 | 39 | 33 | 65 |
| Economic Grain Equivalent | 2,060 | 2,224 | 2,985 | 2,544 | 5,041 |

| % Increase | 1965-1980 | 1965-2000 | 1980-2000* |
|---|---|---|---|
| Total Food Supplies | 45 | 144 | 68 |
| Animal Food Supplies | 50 | 174 | 83 |

| % Annual rates of increase (compound) | | | |
|---|---|---|---|
| Total Food Supplies | 2.5 | 2.6 | 2.6 |
| Animal Food Supplies | 2.7 | 2.9 | 3.1 |

*After attainment of short-term goal

## References

[1]Sukhatme, P. V.; *The World's Food Supplies;* Food and Agriculture Organization of the United Nations, Rome, 1969, p. 6

[2]*The American Theosophist;* Vol. 55, No. 1, January 1967, pp. 332-3

[3]Boerma, A. H.; *Food Requirements and Production Possibilities;* United Nations Economic and Social Council (UNESCO), Paris, p. 12

[4]Brown, H., Bonner, J., and Weir, J.; *The Next Hundred Years*; Viking Press, New York, 1957, p. 71

[5]Kuppuswamy, S., Srinivasan, M., and Subrahmanyan, V.; *Proteins in Foods*; Indian Council of Medical Research, New Delhi, 1958

[6]Bean, Louis H.; "Closing the World's Nutritional Gap; speech presented to the Organizational Meeting of the Committee on the World Food Crisis, Washington, D.C., December 9, 1965, pp. 7-8

[7]Altschul, Aaron M.; *Proteins: Their Chemistry and Politics*; Basic Books, New York, 1965, p. 264

[8]Patton, Donald; *The United States and World Resources*; D. Van Nostrand Co., Inc., New Jersey, 1968, p. 112

[9]Kottman, Roy M.; "Animal Agriculture: Meeting the Critical Issues Head On;" *Proceedings: Sixteenth National Institute of Animal Agriculture*; Purdue University, Lafayette, Indiana, April 1966, p. 34

[10]*Feed Situation*; Economic Research Service, U.S.D.A., Washington, D.C., February 1972, pp. 7, 19

[11]*Agriculture in the Developing Countries Within a World Framework*; Food and Agriculture Organization of the United Nations, Rome, 1970, p. 515

[12]Holt, S. J.; "The Food Resources of the Ocean; *Scientific American*; Vol. 221, No. 3, September 1969, p. 178

[13]*FAO Yearbook of Fishery Statistics*; Vol. 29, Fishery Commodities, 1969, p. a-4

[14]MacKenzie, D. S.; *Environmental Quality and the Meat Industry*; The American Meat Institute, Chicago, January 19, 1970, p. 1

[15]"Now It's Beef and Mutton;" *Newsweek*; November 8, 1971, p. 85

[16]*Ibid.*

[17]Altschul; *op. cit.*, p. 265

[18]Bean, Louis H.; *Closing the World's Nutrition Gap*; Committee on the World Food Crisis, Washington, D.C., December 9, 1965, p. 14

[19]U.S.D.A.

[20]Sukhatme, P. V.; *The World Food Supplies*; Food and Agriculture Organization of the United Nations, Rome, 1969, p. 20

[21]*Ibid.*, p. 22

Chapter 6

# A VEGETARIAN DIET CAN SAVE YOU MONEY

Animals are my friends,
and I don't eat my friends.
—Rukmini Devi Arundale

It is sometimes argued that a vegetarian diet is more expensive than an ordinary meat diet, but in reality this is not the case. In fact, a varied, imaginative, and healthful meat-free diet can cut the average food bill by more than fifty per cent, and can supply a family with an exciting variety of delicious and wholesome casseroles, loaves, soups, stews, and salads to enjoy.

Vegetarians do not, as is generally supposed, consume large quantities of expensive vegetables, fruits and nuts. On the contrary, the trend is toward the more simple and less costly food, which can supply the normal human with more than enough of his daily nutritional needs.

As nutritionists have told us, the real value of food lies in its nutritional value. In the following table we will compare the general nutritive value of a number of popular foods which are obtained from both the animal and vegetable kingdoms:

Table 6-1

**COMPARABLE FOOD VALUES OF EDIBLE PORTIONS, 100 GRAMS[1]**

| Food | % Water | Grams Protein | Grams Fat | Grams Carbo-hydrate | Energy Value (calories) |
|---|---|---|---|---|---|
| Beef, round | 66.6 | 20.2 | 12.3 | 0 | 197 |
| Lamb, loin | 59.3 | 16.8 | 22.6 | 0 | 276 |
| Chicken (fryer) | 75.7 | 18.6 | 4.9 | 0 | 124 |
| Cheese, cheddar | 37.0 | 25.0 | 32.2 | 2.1 | 398 |
| Soybeans (dry, raw) | 10.0 | 34.1 | 17.7 | 33.5 | 403 |
| Lentils (dry, raw) | 11.1 | 24.7 | 1.1 | 60.1 | 340 |
| Garbanzos (dry, raw) | 10.7 | 20.5 | 4.8 | 61.0 | 360 |
| Peanuts | 5.6 | 26.0 | 47.5 | 18.6 | 564 |
| Almonds | 4.7 | 18.6 | 52.4 | 19.5 | 598 |
| Cow's Milk (whole, powdered) | 2.0 | 26.4 | 27.5 | 38.2 | 502 |
| Soybean Milk (whole, powdered) | 4.2 | 41.8 | 20.3 | 28.0 | 429 |

Since meat contains high percentages of water, and less than a comparable amount of protein, it is obvious that pound per pound meat is a poor value for the money, especially when compared with the high protein vegetarian foods.

The information provided in the following tables was based on May 1972 prices at large supermarkets located in the Los Angeles, New York, and Chicago metropolitan areas.

Table 6-2

**TYPICAL PRICES OF MEAT: MAY, 1972**

| Product | Pounds | No. Portions | Price | Cost per lb. | Approx cost per serving |
|---|---|---|---|---|---|
| Top Sirloin Steak | 2 | 4 | $3.42 | $1.71 | 85¢ |
| Lamb Chops (loin) | 2 | 4 | 3.96 | 1.98 | 99¢ |
| Halibut Steak | 1 | 4 | 1.49 | 1.49 | 37¢ |
| Pork Chops (loin) | 1-1/3 | 4 | 1.45 | 1.09 | 36¢ |
| Ham (boneless, smoked) | 3 | 8 | 4.41 | 1.47 | 55¢ |
| Chopped Meat (beef) | 2 | 8 | 1.42 | .71 | 18¢ |
| Chopped Meat (chuck) | 2 | 8 | 1.96 | .98 | 25¢ |
| Chicken Fryer (cut up) | 3 | 4 | 1.20 | .40 | 30¢ |
| Frankfurters | 4/5 | 4 | .70 | .87 | 17¢ |
| Pot Roast | 3½ | 8 | 4.69 | 1.34 | 59¢ |
| Veal Cutlet | 1 | 3-4 | 2.96 | 2.96 | 74-98¢ |
| Haddock (frozen) | 1 | 4 | 1.09 | 1.09 | 27¢ |
| Pork Sausage | 4/5 | 4 | .76 | .95 | 19¢ |

Table 6-3

**TYPICAL PRICES OF NATURAL MEAT SUBSTITUTES**

| Product | Pounds | No. Portions | Price per lb. | Approx. Cost per serving |
|---|---|---|---|---|
| Cooking Soybeans (dry) (health food store) | 1 | 9 | 37¢ | 4¢ |
| Split Peas (dry) | 1 | 9 | 15¢ | 1½¢ |
| Lentils (dry) | 1 | 9 | 21¢ | 2¢ |
| Brown Rice | 1 | 9 | 35¢ | 4¢ |
| Great Northern Beans | 1 | 9 | 21¢ | 2¢ |
| Peanuts (toasted in shell) | 1 | 8 | 59¢ | 7¢ |
| Peanuts (shelled, raw, organic) | 1 | 8 | 59¢ | 7¢ |
| Oats | 1 | 8-12 | 30¢ | 2-4¢ |
| Wheat Germ (super- market, toasted) | 1 | — | 60¢ | — |
| Wheat Germ (organic, raw) | 1 | — | 52¢ | — |
| Sunflower Seeds (shelled, organic) | 1 | 8 | 64¢ | 8¢ |
| Peanut Butter (supermarket) | 1 | — | 65¢ | — |

In the following table we compare the cost of usable protein which the average person obtains from meat, fish, dairy products, grains, and other high protein vegetable sources. The information was based on estimates from *Diet for a Small Planet,* a Friends of the Earth/Ballantine

Book. Please note that 43.1 grams of usable protein (protein which can be assimilated into the human body) is the daily protein allowance for the average 154 pound American male.

### Table 6-4

**PROTEIN COST COMPARISONS**

| Product | Price per Pound | Cost of 43.1 grams usable protein |
|---|---|---|
| **MEATS:** | | |
| Hamburger, regular, ground | $ .63 | $ .51 |
| Pork Loin Chop (medium, fat, w/bone) | 1.09 | 1.15 |
| Porterhouse Steak (choice, w/bone) | 1.58 | 1.67 |
| Lamb Rib Chop (choice, w/bone) | 1.49 | 1.81 |
| **FISH:** | | |
| Swordfish | .79 | .34 |
| Tuna (canned in oil) | .96 | .48 |
| Sardines | .85 | .56 |
| **DAIRY PRODUCTS:** | | |
| Dried Nonfat Milk Solids | .39 | .10 |
| Cottage Cheese (from skimmed milk) | .31 | .19 |
| Whole Milk | .26 (quart) | .44 |
| Cheddar Cheese | 1.13 | .62 |
| Yogurt (from skimmed milk) | .44 | 1.52 |
| Dried Soybean Milk (included for comparison) | .34 | .08 |
| **LEGUMES:** | | |
| Soybeans, Soygrits and Soyflour | .33 | .15 |
| Blackeye Peas | .16 | .16 |
| Split Peas | .19 | .19 |
| Garbanzos | .25 | .27 |
| Lentils | .23 | .31 |
| **GRAINS, CEREALS, AND THEIR PRODUCTS:** | | |
| Whole Wheat Flour | .19 | .21 |
| Rye Flour (dark) | .22 | .22 |
| Wheat Germ | .47 | .27 |
| Oatmeal | .28 | .28 |
| Brown Rice | .21 | .38 |
| Whole Wheat Bread (supermarket variety) | .38 | .66 |
| **NUTS AND SEEDS:** | | |
| Peanut Butter | .61 | .54 |
| Peanuts (raw) | .66 | .57 |
| Sunflower Seeds | .90 | .62 |
| Cashews (raw) | 1.31 | 1.30 |
| Brewer's Yeast | 1.20 | .54 |

In summary, we can now see that a carefully selected vegetarian diet can be high in nutritive value, and be inexpensive at the same time.

Here are several useful suggestions which can help the consumer get the most value out of a shrinking food dollar:

— Raw foods in their natural state are always cheaper and more wholesome than prepared, processed, and packaged food products.

— Home baked bread made with whole grain flour tastes better, remains free of chemical additives, and will be much less expensive than the devitalized, preserved supermarket breads.

— A garden can supply an enormous quantity of wholesome and delicious food at a fraction of the cost of the store bought variety.

— Sprouted beans is a project which can be undertaken indoors. High protein sprouts taste good, are very inexpensive, and can be used in dozens of interesting and delicious vegetarian dishes.

— A listing of several excellent vegetarian cookbooks, as well as other recommended reading material is included in the appendices at the end of this book.

### References

[1] Watt, B. K. & Merrill, A. L.; *Composition of Foods;* Agricultural Handbook No. 8, United States Department of Agriculture, Washington, D.C., 1963, pp. 6-67

[2] Lappé, Frances Moore; *Diet for a Small Planet*; Ballantine Books, New York, 1971, pp. 272-4

## Section 2

In the preceding section of this book we have dealt with the material, self-oriented aspects of vegetarianism which directly affect each and every human being. It has been shown that from a perspective of history, comparative anatomy, health, strength, ecology and economy, a vegetarian diet is not just a passing stage of food faddism, but rather a proven, practical and sensible way of living.

In this second section, another aspect of vegetarianism is to be considered; many feel this is even more meaningful and vital than the physical and other material reasons: our responsibility towards nature.

## Chapter 7

# THE SIN OF THE SLAUGHTERHOUSE

Man is the only animal that
blushes, or needs to.

—Mark Twain

As our society has become more standardized, super-
ficial and mechanized, many of us, through years of conditioning, have grown apart from Nature and her living
creatures which share this planet with us.

This conditioning has helped produce a strong feeling
of callousness on our part in our dealings with other members of the animal kingdom. This is evidenced by the
prevailing belief that we as human beings are literally in
charge of the earth, and everything on this planet was
created for our benefit; so we may do anything we wish
with it.

For example, many people have the strange notion that
alligators are born to supply us with pocketbooks and
souvenirs; that sheep are to provide us with lamb chops;
that deer are for hunting; that horses are to be made a
spectacle of at the rodeo; that turkeys are to be raised
so that we may give thanks to God every Thanksgiving and
Christmas by eating their bodies; and that baby seals,
minks, raccoons, beaver and fox are intended to be speared,
clubbed, shot, and trapped, so that we can make coats
and hats from their soft fur.

This same thought pattern has also led man to believe
that rivers exist so that he might pump sewage into them;
that the desert is a convenient place for the testing of
atomic bombs, and that forests are there so that man can

go snowmobiling through them or spend the weekend there looking for animals to hunt and kill.

Perhaps the most alarming result of our conditioning is the belief that the animals we eat for dinner walk willingly and quietly to a painless and quick death in what is euphemistically termed a "processing plant" to reappear later as a custom-cut main course packed under cellophane at an air-conditioned supermarket, bearing no resemblance whatsoever to the animal from which it originally came.

The facts of the matter are very different from such wishful thinking. As the sun passes over North America every morning, a wave of slaughter begins. In the United States alone, nearly nine million creatures are slaughtered daily for our supposed dietary needs. In a recent year, more than three billion two hundred eighty million cattle, calves, sheep, lambs, hogs, chickens, turkeys and ducks were butchered in this country for our consumption.

If we break this down to specifics, we find that approximately thirty-six million cattle are slaughtered yearly in the United States.[1] This figure is as large as the human population of Louisiana, Oklahoma, Delaware, Maryland, Washington, D.C., West Virginia, Virginia, North Carolina, South Carolina, Mississippi, and Georgia combined!

The number of four-to-six year old calves butchered in the United States in 1971 was 3,821,200[2] and equaled the human population count of Colorado, Montana, New Mexico, Wyoming, and Utah.

More than 10,967,000 sheep and lambs were slaughtered in this country in 1971,[3] which equals the number of all the people living in Chicago, Detroit, Boston, Los Angeles, and New Orleans during the same year.

And if we add up the total number of humans living in the nine most populous states in this country: California, New York, Pennsylvania, Texas, Illinois, Ohio, Michigan, New Jersey and Massachusetts, we would just about equal the 1971 hog slaughter of 95,549,900 animals.[4]

The final United States slaughter includes more than 2,946,294,000 chickens, 105,549,000 turkeys, and

11,833,000 ducks killed during a recent year.[5] The national estimate does not include, however, the yearly slaughter of geese, capons, and other poultry; nonfederally inspected chickens, ducks, and turkeys; nor does it include those creatures which were trapped, gassed, shot, butchered, or clubbed by hunters, fur traders, and vivisectionists. We also did not include the yearly spearing, hooking, and netting of the more than five and a half billion pounds of fish and shellfish which are killed yearly for domestic consumption.[6]

### Table 7-1
**SLAUGHTER OF ANIMALS: CANADA, 1971[7]**

| | |
|---|---:|
| Cattle | 3,299,300 |
| Calves | 763,700 |
| Sheep and Lambs | 441,400 |
| Hogs | 11,550,100 |

(poultry and fish not included)

### Table 7-2
**WORLD SLAUGHTER OF ANIMALS, 1968[8]**

| | |
|---|---:|
| Cattle | 107,023,000 |
| Calves | 26,754,000 |
| Buffaloes | 848,000 |
| Sheep | 111,791,000 |
| Lambs | 63,113,000 |
| Goats and Kids | 7,137,000 |
| Pigs | 278,235,000 |
| Horses | 609,000 |
| Total = | 595,510,000 animals |

(Data are incomplete. These figures do not include the slaughter of poultry, rabbits, wild animals, and fish. In addition, some nations report only government inspected slaughter. Figures do not include reports from several smaller nations, primarily in Africa and Asia, but inspection of the figures for earlier years indicates that the total cited above would be much higher.)

## The Slaughter

Many people misunderstand what is actually involved in the slaughtering of the animals we eat. In the following pages we will briefly survey the mechanics of the slaughtering process, setting aside the more grisly details.

Before the animals are slaughtered they must be transported by rail or truck either to the stockyards or directly to the slaughterhouse. This involves being jammed into a confined area for many hours and sometimes for days. The animals are forced to suffer from lack of ventilation, food and water, and extreme heat, cold, or humidity. When the animals that survive finally reach the holding pens, they are often jabbed with electric prods so that they move faster. For those who underestimate the cattle prod, it is capable of producing first degree burns.[9] By the time the animals are ready for slaughter, they have been kept off feed from 24 to 48 hours.[10]

Before the Federal Humane Slaughter Act went into effect on July 1, 1960, nearly all of the cattle, hogs, calves and lambs killed in the United States were driven into a pen, shackled around one hind leg and then hoisted aloft by a mechanical pulley. If they were cooperative, their throats were immediately slashed with a seven inch knife. If instead the frightened animals thrashed about, they were smashed in the head with either a sledgehammer or pole ax, and then were finally killed with the knife.

Since the Federal Humane Slaughter Act became effective, however, all meat packing companies which do business with the Federal government have been required to stun the animals before slaughter. There are three principal methods of stunning:

In the slaughter of hogs, the animal is forced onto a conveyor belt with an electric prod. This conveyor then takes the hog through a chamber of carbon dioxide gas, which renders the animal unconscious; as it leaves the chamber, it is brought on the belt to the "sticker" whose job is to cut the animal's throat. (Aside from the "humane" aspect, such a method can efficiently kill over one thousand hogs an hour, and is found in only several of the largest slaughterhouses.)

Most of the other large abattoirs employ either a device which gives the animal a high voltage electric shock, or the mechanical stunners, which use either compressed air or a spike which penetrates the skull. These methods are cheaper than gas, and can be used on all classes of livestock.

Most of the smaller slaughterhouses still kill the animals in the same manner which prevailed at the turn of the century: the shackle and hoist, the pole ax, or the rifle.

All animals destined for Kosher consumption are killed by the "Shehitah" method, or Jewish ritual slaughter. This method employs the shackle and hoist, and calls for the animal to be conscious at the moment of slaughter. In theory, this particular method is supposed to be more humane than stunning, and is performed by a trained rabbi who makes a ceremonial knife cut which is supposed to sever the windpipe and jugular vein in one quick incision. In practice, however, the animal may suffer several minutes of agony before it finally bleeds to death, either through the Shehitah method, or with the use of the "humane" stunners:

> Since calves struggle for a longer period after sticking than other classes of livestock, it is well to hoist them before sticking. This keeps them clean and makes it easier to skin out the head and foreshanks.[11]
>
> Do not allow the sheep to kick about and get bloody.[12]

Turkeys, chickens, ducks and geese are killed without the use of stunning. The principal methods of killing include the chopping block method, the cutting of the bird's throat, or by the twisting and breaking of the neck.

\*    \*    \*

Although the individual is conditioned to eat meat by his environment and by society in general, there are other factors involved which encourage us to have animals killed for our dinner. Perhaps the strongest forces behind the nationwide conditioning process are the meat packing interests. From the earliest years of childhood we are coerced into viewing the systematic slaughter of animals as respectable through the subtle and not so subtle efforts of the meat industry.

In addition to the direct advertising by the meat packers themselves, such agencies as the American Meat Institute serve the interests of the industry through an elaborate and expensive public relations campaign which penetrates into all segments of American life. The A.M.I. accomplishes this by ". . . supplying pertinent material in the form of news releases to newspapers, magazines, radio and television stations, and in the form of pamphlets, booklets, charts, posters, and leaflets to schools, libraries, home economists, rural and urban organizations, and thought leaders throughout the nation."[13]

Some of the literature directed toward children is in the form of small booklets. Although they are very attractive and well written, they subtly influence the child to overlook the fact that the hamburger he eats comes from a slaughtered animal. Two of these booklets portray cattle and pigs smiling all the way to the moment of slaughter — a reality which somehow is never actually mentioned. Instead of using the simple words "killed" or "slaughtered" in the text, we find terms like "dispatched," "turned beef on the hoof into meat for the store,"[14] and "turn the pig into eatin' meat."[15] Such strategy encourages the child to avoid reality and sweep "reverence for life" under a carpet of euphemisms.

The Washington, D.C. office, among other activities, maintains a lobby in the Senate and House of Representatives to limit any legislation which can prove dangerous to the interests of the meat packing industry.

The money which the meat industry coins from the

animal kingdom is quite phenomenal; the total value of
sales reported for the United States for 1969 was
$21,875,000,000.00[16] which makes the meat industry con-
stitute the largest sector of the food industry in the United
States.

### Table 7-3

**PER CAPITA CONSUMPTION OF MEAT (in pounds)**

| Item | United States (1969)[17] | Canada (1971)[18] |
|---|---|---|
| Beef | 109.7 | 86.9 |
| Veal | 3.3 | 4.4 |
| Lamb and Mutton | 3.4 | 3.3 |
| Pork | 64.7 | 65.9 |
| Fish | 11.0 | n.a. |
| Offal (entrails, etc.) | n.a. | 4.3 |
| Chicken | 38.9 | 32.9 |
| Turkey | 8.2 | 10.3 |
| Canned Meats (spec. classification) | n.a. | 4.7  (1970) |
| Total (in lbs. per person per year) | 239.2 | 212.7 (excluding fish) |

### Table 7-4

**ESTIMATED NUMBER OF ANIMALS SLAUGHTERED FOR
NORMAL HUMAN BEING DURING 70 YEAR LIFETIME[19]**

| | |
|---|---|
| Cattle | 14 eaten during lifetime |
| Calves | 2 eaten during lifetime |
| Lambs, Sheep | 12 eaten during lifetime |
| Hogs | 23 eaten during lifetime |
| Turkeys | 35 eaten during lifetime |
| Chickens | 840 eaten during lifetime |
| Fish | 770 pounds |

*References*

[1]*Livestock Slaughter 1971*; Statistical Reporting Service, U.S.D.A., Washington, D.C., 1972, p. 5

[2]*Ibid.*, p. 6

[3]*Ibid.*, p. 7

[4]*Ibid.*, p. 9

[5]*Agricultural Statistics 1971*; Statistical Reporting Service, U.S.D.A., Washington, D.C., 1971, p. 423

[6]*Statistical Abstract of the United States 1970*; U.S. Department of Commerce, Washington, D.C., 1970, p. 638

[7]*Statistics Canada*; Ministry of Industry, Trade and Commerce, Ottawa, 1972, p. 3

[8]*FAO Production Yearbook*; Vol. 23, United Nations Food and Agriculture Organization, Rome, 1969, pp. 366-73

[9]Morse, Mel; *Ordeal of the Animals*; Prentice Hall Inc., Englewood Cliffs, N.J., 1968, p. 65

[10]Ziegler, P. Thomas; *The Meat We Eat*; The Interstate Publishers and Printers Inc., Danville, Ill., 1966, p. 64

[11]*Ibid.*, p.116

[12]*Ibid.*, p. 100

[13]*All About the AMI*; The American Meat Institute, Chicago, p. 13

[14]*The Story of Beef*; The American Meat Institute, Chicago, pp. 4, 10

[15]*The Story of Pork*; The American Meat Institute, Chicago, p. 16

[16]*Meatfacts '71*; The American Meat Institute, Chicago, 1971, p. 22

[17]*Statistical Abstract of the U.S. 1970*; U.S. Department of Commerce, Washington, D.C., 1970, p. 83

[18]*Statistics Canada*; Ministry of Industry, Trade and Commerce, Livestock and Animal Products Section, Ottawa, 1972, p. 2

[19]Based on information concerning meat consumption published in *Statistical Abstract,* and figures of dressed weight of animals taken from *The Meat We Eat,* pp. 28, 54, 63, 107, 113

Chapter 8

# RIGHTS FOR THE ANIMALS?

All life is one
and even the humblest forms
enshrine divinity.

—Anonymous

Through the facts presented in the preceding chapter, one begins to awaken to the unnecessary harm we are doing to our fellow creatures. As a so-called "civilized" people, and as members of a society in search for lasting peace in the world, we cannot remain callous to our responsibility toward nature and insensitive to the inherent rights of all the animals.

> Every religion has taught that man should put himself always on the side of the will of God in the world, on the side of good as against evil, or evolution as against retrogression. The man who ranges himself on the side of evolution realizes the wickedness in destroying life. . . . He knows that the life behind the animal is the Divine Life, that all life in the world is divine; the animals therefore are truly our brothers . . . and we can have no sort of right to take their lives for the gratification of our . . . tastes — no right to cause them untold agony and suffering. . . .[1]
> —The Rt. Rev. Charles W. Leadbeater

It has been argued, however, that because everything down to a virus is living, we are killing most of what we eat. Recent studies have found that plants sense that we are going to cut them, and tomatoes are said to scream when sliced. With every breath that we take, we are killing thousands of tiny organisms. We are actually living through killing, just as nature destroys in order to create. For many vegetarians, these facts cause deep concern, and many meat eaters, while denying that animals have emotions, souls and rights, nevertheless eagerly point out the apparent contradiction in the eating of plants.

It is a fact of life that our present stage of evolution calls for the eating of plants in order to survive. As seen in a previous chapter, the natural diet of man comes directly from the plant kingdom, as we are anatomically suited to a diet of vegetables, fruits, grains, and nuts. Until we are able to receive our nutritional requirements directly from the sun, we will have to take our nutriment from the plant kingdom, thus doing the least possible amount of harm to sentient beings. It is also a fact that the vegetarian eats fewer plants in his lifetime than a meat eater does, because the animals which the meat eater has for dinner consumed thousands of pounds of plant food in order to reach slaughter weight.

Indeed, there is a vast amount of difference between the modest amount of harm involved in obtaining the grains, fruits, vegetables and nuts which are absolutely essential for our survival, and the systematic slaughter of millions of cattle, pigs, lambs and chickens every year which we can easily do without. H. Jay Dinshah of the American Vegan Society expanded on this point in the August, 1971 edition of *Ahimsa*:

> . . . To anyone who believes that life itself has some purpose—or is even its own reason for being—one should not wantonly destroy even plants. The destruction of any life is thus an act not to be taken lightly, or presumed to be isolated in the scheme of things. It is to be preceded by careful consideration of the responsibilities and the possible alternatives involved, and accompanied by an understanding that one is indeed doing the right thing according to his present state of existence. . . . The ethical vegetarian is seriously interested in lessening the suffering that he may be causing in the world—even inadvertently inflicted upon relatively low forms of life.[2]

Other individuals have pointed out that a plant is not killed when it is cut from the source from which it was nourished (such as the stem, root, or soil) in the same sense that an animal dies when its throat is cut. Foods such as the banana, squash, pear, carrot and almond retain their life force (prana) for many days and even months after harvest. In fact, they remain alive until they rot. It is also important to note that seeds and fruits are gathered at the point between the death of the old and the birth of the new. Moreover, these seeds are produced in immense abundance, and only one is needed to replace the original plant.

A famous author once compared the results of burying an apple and a dead sheep. The animal would rot and completely decompose, while the apple would take seed and eventually grow into a strong tree bearing hundreds of delicious apples. He then asked, "Would you rather eat living food or dead food?"

One of the moral arguments against meat eating is that we should permit all beings to live out their respective life cycles, thus affording them the opportunity to experience a full life, just as we would expect for ourselves. With this thought in mind, some vegetarians prefer to eat their fruits and vegetables only at the point of ripeness, when the cycle of life is complete.

### References

[1]Leadbeater, C. W.; *Vegetarianism and Occultism*; The Theosophical Publishing House, Madras, India, 1970, p. 34
[2]"What About Killing Plants?"; *Ahimsa*; August 1971, pp. 6-7

Chapter 9

## QUESTIONS AND ANSWERS

The only way to live is to let live.
—Mahatma K. Gandhi

There are no sound scientific or ethical arguments in favor of meat eating. However, there are several questions that vegetarians are asked, and are expected to answer. The following group of questions is representative of such inquiries. They are not fabricated questions, but are based on actual experiences of the author with individuals either in private conversation, or during lectures dealing with vegetarianism.

Q. What would happen to all the animals if everyone became vegetarian? Won't they overrun the world?

A. It is extremely unlikely that everyone will stop eating meat overnight, so the reduction of the livestock population would be a gradual one. Most of the farm animals in this country multiply through forced breeding, so we can be sure that this particular practice would taper off as well.

Q. Isn't it better for an animal to enjoy a short and happy life than no life at all?

A. When we consider this question it is important to take into account that many of the animals produced in the developed countries are raised by cruel and inhumane battery methods which have turned the pastoral farm into an efficient animal factory. In order to produce the most meat at the highest profit, animals are force fed and injected with many chemical feed mixtures and hormones. Such a practice not only destroys their natural habits and instincts, but raises their metabolism and changes their body chemistry. The various methods of crossbreeding have, over many years, produced animals which bear a sorry resemblance to the agile, independent creatures they might have been in their natural state, if permitted to flourish in small numbers.

As the farms have evolved into animal factories, many animals, especially the pigs and chickens, never see the light of day until they are driven to the slaughterhouse. Their lives are spent in cramped, unnatural surroundings which culminate in a cruel and brutal death in a slaughterhouse. Calves are taken from their mothers before they are a day old[1] and live for only 6 to 10 weeks before they are butchered for veal. Since most people place a premium on light meat, many calves are kept immobilized and fed a mixture which is designed to produce anemia.

Other instances of cruel treatment were published in the book *Animal Machines*:

> At another farm the calves stood in a row on a slatted platform, their heads held between two vertical wooden bars so that they could slide up and down but nothing else. They could slide down to a lying position, but their heads would be relentlessly held; they would have only that one position of rest throughout their lives.[2]

> A large proportion of laying hens and rabbits are kept in tiers of battery cages, their feet having only wire mesh on which to rest.[3]

These are several of many factors which are characteristic of battery farming, and present the question as to whether it is better for an animal to live a life of suffering and degradation or not to be born at all.

Q. Since animals are more highly evolved than plants, it makes sense to eat the animals, so that we in turn can speed up our own evolution.

A. If this idea were carried a bit further, we should legalize cannibalism! In fact, some people feel that the eating of animals actually helps to encourage violence and brutality; two factors which hold man back in his evolutionary journey.

> . . . All pain acts as a record against humanity and slackens and retards the whole of human growth; for you cannot separate yourself in that way from the world, you cannot isolate yourself and go on in evolution yourself while you are trampling others down. Those that you trample on retard your own progress. The misery that you cause is as it were mire which clings round your feet when you would ascend; for we have to rise together or fall together, and all the misery we inflict on sentient beings slackens our human evolution and makes the progress of humanity slower towards the ideal that it is seeking to realize.[4]
>
> —Annie Besant

Q. But I like the taste of meat. I just couldn't do without a juicy steak!

A. Similar statements are made by those addicted to cigarettes and alcohol in support of their respective habits. Meat eating is also a habit, having been reinforced by many years of conditioning and propaganda. Most people are so conditioned by what they are told over the years, they are often afraid to break down the old patterns in favor of a more independent, sensible and humane alternative.

The time is long overdue for those human beings who call themselves "civilized" to look with disdain on the unnecessary and unnatural practice of subjugating innocent animals, like cows, pigs and lambs, to odious torture and violent death simply because "they taste good." The carnivorous animals of the world kill for survival. Man is the only animal that destroys all other species, and even his own, for pleasure and greed.

Besides being healthy and nutritious, fruits, nuts, and vegetables taste delicious in their own right, although an intelligent person should consider factors other than taste when selecting a diet. Many vegetarians have found that their taste buds actually become more sensitive after abandoning a meat diet. No medical evidence has been presented which has supported this claim, but if the meat eater wishes to test his own conditioning, a thirty day abstention from flesh food is invited. After the thirty day trial period, he should eat some meat and see how it affects him.

Q. But man has eaten meat for thousands of years. It's the tradition.

A. The existence of a practice does not justify it, especially if it causes harm to others. If it were so, we could easily rationalize murder, rape, and theft, since men have been guilty of these practices for thousands of years.

The fact that a million people commit a crime does not make it less of a crime. It is important to learn how to think for oneself and not believe that a certain practice is correct because it is the custom or because it is viewed as respectable by society.

Q. This may be true, but why hasn't my doctor recommended a vegetarian diet?

A. It has been pointed out by some that the state of the medical profession today is often one of the blind leading the blind. The doctor and his family suffer from the same diseases as everyone else, and oftentimes partake in the same unhealthy practices as the general public, such as smoking and drinking. Since childhood, the doctor has usually been heavily conditioned along certain lines of behavior, especially in regard to the belief that one can't be healthy without eating large amounts of meat and other animal products. Even in medical school one is generally taught how to treat the results rather than to eliminate the underlying factors which cause disease in the first place.

Of course this is not true in every instance, and there are surely many informed, dedicated and selfless physicians who are highly interested in preventive medicine. Nevertheless it can be seen that today there appears to be more disease, more pills, more hopsitals, more research and more surgery than ever before. It would seem that all of modern medicine and established nutritional science haven't come up with the right answers.

It would be sensible, therefore, to begin to think for yourself about these matters. Learn the facts and draw your own conclusions using an inquiring, open mind and above all, common sense.

**References**

[1]*The Dairyman*; January 1972, p. 26
[2]Harrison, Ruth; *Animal Machines*; Ballantine Books, New York, 1966, p. 87
[3]*Ibid.*, pp. 112D, 112E
[4]Besant, Annie; *Vegetarianism in the Light of Theosophy*; The Theosophical Publishing House, Madras, India, 1919, pp. 18-19

## Chapter 10

# VEGETARIANISM: NOT AN END IN ITSELF

One sees things in fragments and thinks in fragments.
We must inquire into what it means to see totally.

—J. Krishnamurti

Some people feel that the answer to the problems of the world lies in the vegetarian diet. Such a belief is only partly true, although it is a fact that many religions and men such as Jesus, Gautama Buddha and Gandhi have emphasized the use of a vegetarian diet in their teachings.

If one wishes to consider the whole panorama of life, he can see that the adoption of a harmless diet is but the first step of many which lead to an individual in harmony with himself in a world at peace.

At the present time we are living in a world steeped in violence and hatred. More than one billion of its citizens are suffering from lack of an adequate diet, while a minority of the population is rapidly depleting the world of its most valuable resources: clean water and arable land. Those who live in the more developed countries such as the United States, are faced with the increasing threat of heart disease, stomach disorders, obesity, and a myriad of other physical ailments; many are forced to spend much of their adult lives as semi-invalids. At the same time, people cry out "stop the killing" in their quest for world peace, while billions of animals are being brutally slaughtered for their dinner. Human beings are drifting away from the land, and most have but a dim vision about where their food comes from.

A vegetarian diet can be an answer to many of these problems. A regimen of wholesome fruits, grains, nuts, and vegetables can do much in the field of ecology, and can help to eliminate the world food shortage. The non-meat diet has also proven itself to be conducive to good health, and to provide the foundation for a vital, active life. A vegetarian diet also does the least amount of harm to other living things, and if one respects some of the living creatures with whom we share this planet, there is a higher degree of respect for all beings. Then one can truly help to stop killing, and apply one's ideals to daily living.

The adoption of a healthy, harmless, and economically sound diet does not depend on what the neighbors think, nor on what society says or does; it is the genuine resolution to govern one's life according to compassion, kindness, and reverence for all beings.

The change to a vegetarian diet is a first step to help ease the suffering in the world, for it is in tune with the unity of all life, and conforms to the kind of diet which is naturally intended for man.

> O Hidden Life, Vibrant in Every Atom
> O Hidden Light, Shining in Every Creature
> O Hidden Love, Embracing All in Oneness,
>
> May each who feels himself as One with Thee
> Know he is therefore One with every other.

> OM     Shanti     OM

# Section 3

## Chapter 11

## SCIENTIFIC NUTRITION

The body is your animal—
the horse upon which you ride.
Therefore you must treat it well,
and take good care of it.

*—At the Feet of the Master*

The important and complex subject of human nutrition cannot possibly be adequately studied in one chapter. Nevertheless, the writer feels that a book about vegetarianism would not be complete without an attempt to include a concise and practical guide to achieving optimum health from a meat free diet.

There are many components to sound nutrition, and several of these factors have very little to do with eating the proper foods. In understanding good nutrition we must consider the factors of environment, the inherent psychological and emotional state of the individual, the physical condition of the body, the habits which the individual has acquired in life and so on. However, for the sake of brevity we will concentrate our efforts on the "food" section of the nutrition panorama, and as in previous chapters, we will utilize the findings of competent scientists and responsible specialists who are experts in their respective fields.

### *Part 1 — What is Nutrition?*

In undertaking this survey, it would be of value to view briefly what is actually involved in the nutritional process. Dr. Herbert M. Shelton, nationally known health educator and leader in the hygienic movement, defines nutrition in this way:

> Nutrition is the cardinal function of organic evolution and growth. It is the sum of all processes by which raw materials (footstuffs) are transformed into living structure and prepared for use by the body. It is the appropriation of nutritive material . . . by the plant or animal and its transformation into cell substance and structural units. It is the means by which food is transformed in the case of plants, into sap, pulp, woody fiber, leaf, flower, fruit, and seed, and in the case of animals, into blood, muscle, bone, nerve, and gland.[1]

Dr. Shelton also outlines the means by which the body appropriates its food:

A. *Substances Appropriated:*
(1) Food     (2) Air (oxygen)     (3) Water
(4) Sunshine

B. *Ways of Appropriation:*
(1) Locomotion    (2) Prehension    (3) Mastication
(4) Deglutation    (5) Digestion     (6) Absorption
(7) Respiration     (8) Circulation    (9) Assimilation

C. *Results of Appropriation:*
(1) Development    (2) Growth     (3) Repair
(4) Maintenance    (5) Healing    (6) Reproduction[2]

## Eating

As we mentioned earlier, food consumption alone does not necessarily imply total nutrition, but it is nonetheless true that the food we eat plays a most decisive role in the healthful upkeep of our minds and bodies.

There are three basic reasons for eating and drinking:

(1) To promote growth, especially during our younger years,
(2) To supply fuel needed for energy and heat which is used to operate the physical mechanism,
(3) To maintain the body structure: the bones, tissues, organs, bloodstream, etc., at peak efficiency.

To obtain maximum nutritional and economic value from the foods we consume, we might wish to consider the following suggestions:

— Eat quietly and without rushing. Do not eat when emotionally upset or excited, or when tired or in pain. Try to chew the food thoroughly, since the first stage of the digestive process takes place in the mouth. As a doctor once told me, "The stomach doesn't have teeth." Eat only when hungry, and avoid eating too much food. Overeating puts an unnecessary strain on the body and causes it to function less efficiently.

— If at all possible, avoid processed, devitalized, and chemically treated foods, such as white sugar, sweets, white bread, food mixes, ready-to-serve foods, commercially prepared cereals (except muesli and granola type cereals, which are less refined and more nourishing than most cereals), and other canned, pickled, spiced, preserved, or otherwise adulterated foods. It has been reported that more than 800 million pounds of chemicals are added annually to our food, which means that the average American eats more than three and a half pounds of preservatives, stabilizers, colorants, poison sprays, emollients, and other chemical adulterants per year.[3]

— If it is practical to do so, use organically grown foods, and try to buy foods raw. If you cannot purchase them in their natural state, frozen foods are better than canned foods, though not as good as fresh foods.

The closer the food is to its natural state, the better it tastes, and the greater its nutritional value. There is also much merit in eating foods raw whenever possible, especially in the case of fruits and nuts. Obviously such foods as potatoes, dried beans and dried peas have to be cooked, but it has been found that many other foods lose their nutritional value through prolonged soaking and boiling. If vegetables are to be cooked at all, nutritionists advise steaming, pressure cooking, or baking, as these methods help preserve the essential nutrients of these foods.

The plant kingdom is our source of perfect nourishment. Every essential food element necessary for superior nutrition is available from nonmeat sources. The following sections deal with the subjects of protein, carbohydrates, fats and oils, minerals, and vitamins which are all adequately supplied by vegetarian foods.

## Part 2 — The Protein Question

The word "protein" comes from the Greek word meaning "I stand first." The functions of protein are of prime importance to everyone.

*Protein* —  is essential for growth;
— regulates the body's water balance and maintains the efficient distribution of body fluids to every cell in the organism;
— is needed in the maintenance of body neutrality. Proteins serve as "buffers" capable of reacting with either acids or bases (alkalines); and prevent an imbalance between the two.
— is necessary in combating infection and disease.

### Amino Acids

The amino acids are regarded as the building blocks of protein, and we need to consume nine essential amino acids daily in order to preserve good health.

Drs. W. C. Rose and R. Leverton have reported their findings on each of the essential amino acids required by adult men and women. This minimum can be fulfilled with about four slices of whole wheat bread and one pint (500 gr.) of either cow's milk or soybean milk each day.

## Table 11-1

### DAILY REQUIREMENTS OF ESSENTIAL AMINO ACIDS, in grams.[4]

| Amino Acid | Cow's Milk | Soybean Milk[5] | Whole Wheat Bread | Total | | MDR Rose[6] (Men) | MDR Leverton[7] (Women) |
|---|---|---|---|---|---|---|---|
| | (500 grams) | (100 grams) | | | | | |
| Tryptophan | 0.245 | (0.255) | 0.91 | 0.336 | (0.346) | 0.25 | 0.16 |
| Treonine | 0.805 | (0.880) | 0.282 | 1.090 | (1.162) | 0.50 | 0.31 |
| Isoleucine | 1.115 | (0.875) | 0.429 | 1.540 | (1.304) | 0.70 | 0.45 |
| Leucine | 1.720 | (1.525) | 0.668 | 2.340 | (2.193) | 1.10 | 0.62 |
| Methionine | 0.430 | (0.270) | 0.142 | 0.570 | (0.412) | 1.10 | 0.55 |
| Cystine | 0.155 | (0.355) | 0.200 | 0.360 | (0.555) | — | — |
| Phenyklanine | 0.850 | (0.975) | 0.465 | 1.320 | (1.440) | 1.10 | 0.22 |
| Valine | 1.200 | (0.930) | 0.435 | 1.630 | (1.365) | 0.80 | 0.65 |
| Tyrosine | 0.890 | (0.965) | —— | 0.890 | (0.965) | — | 0.65 |

NOTE: Twice the minimum is what Dr. Rose considers an "absolutely safe" intake.

## Complete and Incomplete Proteins

A great deal of misunderstanding exists in the minds of many regarding complete and incomplete proteins. A complete protein food is one which contains all of the essential amino acids. Meat, dairy products, eggs, most beans, soybeans, whole wheat, and wheat gluten are complete proteins. Most other foods are termed "incomplete," but nevertheless are extremely beneficial for good health. If we choose a food rich in some amino acids and not in others, and then select a complementary food source that supplies us with the other amino acids, we have a complete protein. Dr. Mervyn G. Hardinge, Dean of the Loma Linda University School of Public Health writes:

> From a nutritional point of view animal or vegetable proteins should not be differentiated. . . . The adequacy of the protein intake depends, not on the complexity of any single protein, but on the composition of the mixture of amino acids resulting from the breakdown of all the proteins of the meal.[8]

Such a balance is not so difficult to achieve. This can readily be obtained from any well chosen vegetarian diet, even if it be entirely of plant foods. There is no protein problem when one has access to a wide variety of wholesome plant foods—whole grains, legumes, fruits, and vegetables (especially some green leafy ones). A few nuts or some peanut butter, if these are available, make a good addition, as does a little extra wheat germ. If one uses milk, cheese, and eggs as well, there is certainly no protein problem.

The nonflesh foods which supply high concentrations of protein include soybeans, nuts, cereals, peanuts, whole grains, sunflower seeds, dried peas, wheat germ, sesame seeds, dried beans, brewer's yeast, olives, avocados, soybean milk, cow's milk, eggs, and cheese.

## Protein Deficiency

A deficiency in protein can cause anemia, the inability to resist disease, fatigue, loss of stamina, muscle deterioration, and difficulties in healing bruises and wounds.

Table 11-2

**PROTEIN CONTENT IN FOODS, 100 grams, edible portion[9]**

| Food | Grams protein |
|---|---|
| Cow's Milk (fluid) | 3.5 |
| Soybean Milk (fluid) | 3.4 |
| Peanuts | 26.0 |
| Almonds | 18.6 |
| Avocados | 2.1 |
| Dried Split Peas (cooked) | 8.0 |
| Olives (green) | 1.4 |
| Eggs | 12.9 |
| Cheese (cheddar) | 25.0 |
| Cheese (cottage, uncreamed) | 17.0 |
| Sunflower Seeds | 24.0 |
| Sesame Seeds | 18.4 |
| Wheat Germ | 26.6 |
| Peanut Butter | 27.8 |
| Brown Rice, cooked | 2.5 |
| Brewer's Yeast | 38.8 |
| Soybean Flour (low fat) | 43.4 |

## Minimum Daily Requirement

The minimum daily requirement for protein has been calculated to be

35 grams for a 51 pound, 8 year old child,
55 grams for a 128 pound woman, and
65 grams for a 154 pound man.

## Part 3 — Carbohydrates

### Function

As opposed to proteins, which are the body building and repairing elements, carbohydrates provide us with the heat and energy we need to function each day.

### Sources

The principal sources of carbohydrates include sugar, sweets, all cereals, honey, raisins and other dried fruits, potatoes, macaroni products and dried beans.

> Physiologically, it is best to eat carbohydrates that furnish body building elements—vitamins, minerals, protein—as well as calories [heat and energy units]. This means, eat whole grain cereals, breads, corn-meal, barley, buckwheat and rye, and brown rice in preference to white. It also means minimizing the use of white sugar and its products—candy, syrup, sugary drinks, jelly, jam, and other similar stomach-filling but body-starving concoctions.[10]
>
> —*Food Facts and Fallacies*

*Note:* White sugar is nearly 100% carbohydrate, but is highly refined and robs the body of calcium in the process of being converted into heat. Honey is far superior to white, turbinado, or raw sugar, if these foods are needed at all. "Raw" sugar is merely white sugar with added blackstrap molasses; it is not "natural" but highly refined.

## Minimum Daily Requirements

"Since the body can function with considerably less carbohydrate than is present in most diets, it has been impossible to establish a dietary standard for carbohydrate."[11]

### Part 4 — Fats

## Functions

Fats — produce heat and the energy the body needs daily;
— offer protection from cold and injury (injury to important body organs such as the kidneys) ;
— form long term energy, which is stored in various parts of the body.

## Sources

The principal sources of fat include vegetable oils (safflower, soybean, corn, peanut, cottonseed, olive), milk, eggs, butter, cheese, peanuts and other nuts, avocados, margarine, coconuts, and sunflower and other seeds.

## Saturated versus Unsaturated Fats

Over the years there has been a good deal of controversy regarding this question. In the following paragraphs we will hear from three authoritative sources concerning the subject of fats, none of which, curiously enough, advocates a vegetarian diet.

In *Prevention Method for Better Health* the authors write:

> Animal fats—all of them, including milk, butter, fat meats, lard and so forth—contain cholesterol, the substance that apparently constitutes a grave danger to us since it appears to be responsibe for hardening of the arteries, heart disease, gallstones and so forth. Vegetable fats contain no cholesterol. To take its

place they have sitosterols, which do not act the same way.

Vegetable fat contains, too, what we call unsaturated fatty acids, as opposed to saturated fatty acids that are contained in greater quantity in foods of animal origin. Although there is still considerable debate over the digestibility of fatty foods, we know for certain that the vegetable fats are more easily digested than the animal fats.[12]

The medical textbook, *Proudfit-Robinson's Normal and Therapeutic Nutrition,* discusses the relationship between fats and atherosclerosis:

> Diets that have a liberal proportion of polyunsaturated fatty acids and that are low in saturated fatty acids will lower the blood cholesterol level. Conversely, diets high in saturated fatty acids will lead to an increase in the blood cholesterol.[13]

The authors report that the American Heart Association fat-controlled diet "emphasizes oils high in polyunsaturated fats and sharply restricts those high in saturated fats."[14]

In the second chapter of this book it is shown that the natural diet of man is derived from the plant kingdom. With this in mind, it would seem advisable to use those fats which come from nonanimal sources. In his book *Food is Your Best Medicine,* Henry G. Bieler, M.D. stresses the need for only natural, unadulterated, and unrefined fats in our diets. He encourages the use, therefore, of ". . . vegetable fats, such as the fat in seeds, nuts, avocados, bananas, and other tropical fruits including papayas, mangoes, sapotas, and coconuts."[15]

> But fats, saturated or unsaturated, do their greatest harm to the body when they are used as shortening or cooking oil, that is, when they are heated with other foods, especially the starches. Fried bread or potatoes, doughnuts, hot cakes, pie crust, cakes and pasteries—all offer altered cholesterol. And when you eat these highly regarded confections, the result is imperfect artery lining, erosion of the arteries, atherosclerosis. The greatest offenders are doughnuts and potato chips, and popcorn a close third (before popcorn will "pop" it must be heated in cooking oil.)[16]

*Eating for Life*

## Table 11-3

**SATURATED AND UNSATURATED FATTY ACIDS IN FOODS**
per 100 grams edible portion[17]

| Food | Total Grams saturated fatty acids | Total Grams unsaturated fatty acids |
|---|---|---|
| Meats | | |
| beef | 12 | 12 |
| lamb | 12 | 9 |
| pork | 19 | 27 |
| Cow's Milk | 15 | 10 |
| Soybean Milk | 3 | 15 |
| Cheese | | |
| cheddar | 18 | 12 |
| cream | 21 | 13 |
| cottage | 2 | 1 |
| Poultry and Eggs | | |
| turkey | 4 | 9 |
| chicken | 2 | 3 |
| chicken eggs | 4 | 6 |
| Fish | | |
| herring (Atlantic) | 2 | 2 |
| tuna | 1 | 1 |
| Separated Fats and Oils | | |
| butter | 46 | 29 |
| lard | 38 | 56 |
| corn oil | 10 | 81 |
| soybean oil | 15 | 72 |
| safflower oil | 8 | 87 |
| shortening (animal & vegetable) | 43 | 52 |
| shortening (vegetable) | 23 | 72 |
| margarine | 18-19 | 60-61 |
| olive oil | 11 | 83 |
| Cereals and Grains | | |
| cornmeal, white | trace | 3 |
| millet | 1 | 2 |
| wheat germ | 2 | 8 |
| Fruits and Vegetables (including seeds) | | |
| avocado pulp | 3 | 9 |
| olives (mission) | 2 | 16 |
| sesame seed (whole) | 7 | 40 |
| soybeans (dry) | 3 | 13 |
| Nuts and Peanuts | | |
| almonds | 4 | 47 |
| brazil nuts | 13 | 49 |
| coconut | 30 | 2 |
| cashew | 8 | 35 |
| peanut | 10 | 34 |
| pecan | 5 | 59 |
| walnut (black) | 4 | 49 |

## Minimum Daily Requirement

There is no official United States government minimum daily requirement for fats. However, in the text *Introductory Nutrition* the author writes:

> Nutritionists suggest that an intake of fat providing 25% to 30% of the calories is more compatible with good health.[18]

### Part 5 — Minerals

All foods contain minerals—those body building materials used in the making of bone, muscle, nerve tissue, blood, perspiration, and stomach tissues. Minerals also help with the digestion of foods, and in regulating the temperature of the body.

## A. IRON

### Main Functions:

— To help supply oxygen to the blood
— To help the body resist disease
— To promote red blood cell formation
— To maintain proper metabolism.

### Principal Nonmeat Sources

Whole seeds (such as wheat and oats), raisins, wheat germ, lentils, prunes, dates, apricots, spinach and other green leafy vegetables, dried beans, wholemeal breads, eggs, and brewer's yeast.

Table 11-4

**IRON CONTENT IN FOODS, 100 grams edible portion**[19]

| Food | Iron Content (in milligrams) |
| --- | --- |
| Cabbage | .4 |
| Rolled Oats, cooked | .6 |
| Raisins | 3.5 |
| Wheat Germ | 9.4 |
| Eggs | 2.3 |
| Spinach, cooked | 2.2 |
| Lentils, cooked | 2.1 |
| Lima Beans, cooked | 3.1 |
| Soybeans, cooked | 2.7 |
| Beet Greens, raw | 3.3 |
| Prune Juice | 4.1 |
| Apricots, dried | 5.5 |
| Blackstrap Molasses | 16.1 |
| Brewer's Yeast | 17.3 |

### Minimum Daily Requirements

The minimum daily requirement for iron is 18 milligrams for an adult female and 10 milligrams for an adult male.

## B. *SODIUM*

### *Main Function*

Sodium is found to be very important in the makeup of many of the body fluids. It is found in tears, blood, and perspiration.

### *Sources*

Sodium is found mainly in table salt. However, the average person who performs a normal amount of work does not need table salt, as sodium is naturally provided in celery, cucumbers, green leafy vegetables, apples, berries, nuts, and in dairy produce, especially cheese.

Extra salt should be taken if large amounts of sodium are excreted by sweating in heavy manual work or in very hot climates.

Table 11-5

**SODIUM CONTENT IN FOODS, 100 grams edible portion[20]**

| Food | Sodium Content (in milligrams) |
|---|---|
| Celery | 126 |
| Cucumbers | 6 |
| Grapefruit | 1 |
| Spinach, cooked | 50 |
| Broccoli, cooked | 10 |
| Apples | 1 |
| Prunes, dried | 8-11 |
| Currants, black | 3 |
| Peanuts | 5 |
| Milk, cows, whole | 50 |
| Cheese, cheddar | 700 |
| Eggs, poached | 271 |
| Carrots | 47 |
| Kale | 75 |
| Collards, raw | 43 |

### *Minimum Daily Requirement*

Five grams of sodium daily is said to be adequate for the average person.

## C. CALCIUM

### Main Functions:

- To build bones and teeth
- To help the blood to clot
- To serve as a catalyst in many biological reactions
- To regulate the permeability of the cell membrane
- To regulate the body's intake of Strontium 90, an element contained in radioactive fallout

### Principal Sources

Soybeans, milk and other dairy products, almonds, turnip greens, sesame seeds, dried apricots, kale and spinach.

Table 11-6

**CALCIUM CONTENT IN FOODS, 100 grams edible portion**[21]

| Food | Calcium Content (in milligrams) |
|---|---|
| Soybeans, cooked | 73 |
| Cow's Milk | 118 |
| Soybean Milk | 21 |
| Almonds | 234 |
| Broccoli, cooked | 88 |
| Turnip Greens | 246 |
| Kale | 179 |
| Apricots, dried | 67 |
| Sesame Seeds | 110 |
| Spinach, cooked | 93 |

### Minimum Daily Requirements

The amount of calcium that a person needs daily is 800 milligrams.

## D. *PHOSPHORUS*

### *Principal Functions*

- To regulate the release of energy resulting from the "burning" of proteins
- To give rigidity to the bones and teeth
- Phosphorus is indispensable to all living and growing tissue
- To help make up the essential body compound

### *Main Sources*

Whole grain cereal products, cheese, nuts, eggs, beans, dark green leafy vegetables, root vegetables, dried fruits.

### Table 11-7

**PHOSPHORUS CONTENT IN FOODS, 100 grams edible portion**[22]

| Food | Phosphorus Content (in milligrams) |
|---|---|
| Whole Wheat Bread, toasted | 302 |
| Eggs | 205 |
| Cashews | 373 |
| Soybeans, cooked | 191 |
| Brussels Sprouts, cooked | 72 |
| Spinach | 38 |
| Rutabagas | 39 |
| Dried Prunes | 79 |
| Cheese, American | 771 |
| Peanuts | 401 |

### *Minimum Daily Requirements*

The Food and Nutrition Board of the National Research Council suggests that the phosphorus intake should be at least equal to that of calcium during the period of childhood and during the latter part of pregnancy and lactation. Phosphorus is so widely distributed that the intake of phosphorus in our daily foods usually exceeds that of calcium. . .[23]

## E. IODINE

### Main Functions

— To produce normal action in the thyroid gland, which regulates body metabolism
— Aids in the growth and development of the physical organism

### Principal Sources

Radishes, turnips, spinach, sea kelp, eggs and dairy products, iodized salt.

Table 11-8

**AVERAGE IODINE CONTENT IN FOODS, 100 grams edible portion**[24]

| Food | Iodine Content (in micrograms) |
| --- | --- |
| Vegetables | 28.0 |
| Eggs | 14.5 |
| Dairy Products | 13.9 |
| Bread and Cereal | 10.5 |
| Fruits | 1.8 |

### Minimum Daily Requirement

One microgram of iodine per kilogram (2.2 pounds) of body weight is recommended for adults.

Other trace minerals include magnesium, chlorine, potassium, sulfur, copper, zinc, flourine, and cobalt. As long as a good variety of wholesome foods is eaten, there is no danger of deficiency. If the main mineral requirements are met, the minimal needs of these minerals will be met as well.

## Part 6 — *Vitamins*

Vitamins are not foods, but make the food we eat usable to the body for proper functioning. They are described as a group of food substances which are essential to normal metabolism. Vitamins are present in very small amounts in most foods, and if they are lacking from one's diet a large variety of deficiency diseases can result.

Vitamins are classified in two categories: those which are fat soluble, and those which are water soluble. The fat soluble vitamins are easily dissolved in fat, and those which are water soluble can be dissolved in water. In the case of the water soluble vitamins, it is important to avoid boiling the foods which contain them, or this boiling action will cause the food to lose its nutritional value.

## A. *VITAMIN A (Fat Soluble)*

### *Functions*

- Promotes growth and general nutrition
- Prevents night blindness and diseases of the eye
- Preserves health of the skin
- Helps maintain the well-being of the respiratory tract, and throat, and the bronchial area

### *Primary Sources*

Carrots, spinach, sweet potatoes, broccoli, squash and other yellow and dark green leafy vegetables, butter and margarine.

Table 11-9

**VITAMIN A CONTENT IN FOODS, 100 grams edible portion**[25]

| Food | Vitamin A Content (in International Units) |
|---|---|
| Carrots, raw | 11,000 |
| Spinach, cooked | 8,100 |
| Sweet Potatoes (baked) | 8,100 |
| Broccoli, cooked | 2,500 |
| Kale, cooked | 7,400 |
| Beet Greens, cooked | 5,100 |
| Cress | 9,300 |
| Winter Squash, baked | 4,200 |
| Butter | 3,300 |
| Milk | 140 |

### *Minimum Daily Requirement*

5000 International Units of Vitamin A are recommended daily for a normal adult.

### *Deficiencies*

Deficiencies of this vitamin can cause night blindness, changes in the eye, retarded growth, general weakness, hardening of the skin cells, problems of the respiratory tract, genitourinary tract, gastrointestinal tract, nervous tissue, and tooth enamel.

## B. *THE B VITAMINS (Water Soluble)*

The "B" group of vitamins has been found in recent years to be of tremendous value and importance for every human being. Vitamin B is necessary in the body for maintaining proper digestion and the efficient use of fuel foods. These B vitamins are also needed in the breaking down of proteins so that they can be used effectively in the body, as well as to aid body growth and the proper maintenance of the nervous system.

All of the B vitamins are water soluble, which means that they can lose their potency through prolonged soaking or boiling. In such cases, the soaking or cooking water should be utilized in order to obtain maximum value from foods rich in these important vitamins.

### *Minimum Daily Requirements*

The minimum daily requirements of the B vitamins are included in the sections which follow, along with a listing of the amounts of these vitamins contained in selected foods.

*Note:* The B Vitamins must be taken in proportionate amounts: For example a person who consumes a minimum amount of Vitamin $B_1$ must have a proportionate intake of Vitamin $B_6$ in order to prevent any deficiency.

## 1. *VITAMIN B₁ (THIAMIN)*

### *Functions*

— Adjusts blood pressure and activates nerves
— Aids in the release of energy from carbohydrates
— Helps maintain the body's metabolic rate

### *Main Sources*

Wheat germ, whole cereal products, peas and other legumes, whole wheat bread, dried brewer's yeast, brown rice, dairy products.

Table 11-10

**THIAMIN CONTENT IN FOODS, 100 grams edible portion**[20]

| Food | Thiamin Content (in milligrams) |
|---|---|
| Wheat Germ | 2.01 |
| Whole Wheat Flour | .66 |
| Rolled Oats, cooked | .08 |
| Peanuts, raw | 1.14 |
| Green Peas, cooked | .28 |
| Lentils, cooked | .07 |
| Soybeans, cooked | .21 |
| Milk | .03 |
| Dried Brewer's Yeast | 15.61 |

### *Minimum Daily Requirements*

It is recommended that an adult female consume 1.0 milligrams and an adult male 1.4 milligrams of Vitamin B₁ every day.

### *Deficiencies*

A deficiency of this vitamin can cause abdominal pains, heart irregularities, muscle tenderness, emotional instability, constipation, and irritability.

## 2. *VITAMIN B₂ (RIBOFLAVIN)*

### *Function*

The primary function of Vitamin B₂ is connected with the energy chain processes.

### *Principal Sources*

Wheat germ, dried brewer's yeast, milk, eggs, leafy vegetables, almonds, whole cereals. (*Note:* Cooking and heat do not harmfully affect the value of this vitamin.)

Table 11-11

**RIBOFLAVIN CONTENT IN FOODS, 100 grams edible portion**[27]

| Food | Riboflavin Content (in milligrams) |
|------|-----------------------------------|
| Wheat Germ | .68 |
| Milk | .17 |
| Eggs | .30 |
| Spinach | .14 |
| Almonds | .92 |
| Soybeans | .09 |
| Peanuts, raw | .13 |
| Whole Wheat Bread | .15 |
| Brewer's Yeast, dried | 4.28 |

### *Minimum Daily Requirements*

The recommended minimum daily requirement for this vitamin is 1.5 milligrams for an adult female and 1.7 milligrams for an adult male.

### *Deficiencies*

Deficiencies in Vitamin B₂ include the inflammation of the mouth and lips, smooth purplish tongue, dry and scaly skin, and retarded growth.

### 3. *VITAMIN B₃ (NIACIN)*

#### *Main Functions*

- Plays an important role in the release of energy from carbohydrates, fats, and proteins,
- Is connected with the general growth of the body,
- Called the "morale-boosting" vitamin,
- Aids in maintaining healthy gums.

#### *Primary Sources*

Brewer's yeast, wheat germ, peanuts, lentils, mushrooms, peanut butter; nuts other than peanuts are fair sources, and milk and eggs have niacin equivalent.

Table 11-12

**NIACIN CONTENT IN FOODS, 100 grams edible portion**[28]

| Food | Niacin Content (in milligrams) |
|------|--------------------------------|
| Wheat Bran | 21.0 |
| Peanuts | 17.2 |
| Lentils | 2.0 |
| Lima Beans | 1.3 |
| Peanut Butter | 15.7 |
| Brewer's Yeast, dried | 37.9 |
| Avocados | 1.6 |
| Almonds | 3.5 |
| Mushrooms, raw | 4.2 |

#### *Minimum Daily Requirements*

The recommended minimum daily requirement for niacin has been set at 15 milligrams for a woman and 18 milligrams for an adult male.

#### *Deficiencies*

A deficient intake of Vitamin B₃ can lead to abnormalities in the digestive tract, mental dullness and depression, and pellagra.

## 4. VITAMIN B₆ (PYRIDOXINE)

### Functions

— Produces antibodies to ward off disease
— Maintains healthy skin
— Works toward maintaining the protein and fatty acid metabolism

### Sources

Most vegetables, especially cabbage, spinach, potatoes and lima beans; bananas, brewer's yeast, wheat germ, whole grain cereals, egg yolk, rice bran.

Table 11-13

**AVERAGE VITAMIN B₆ CONTENT OF FOODS,**
**100 grams edible portion[29]**

| Food | Vitamin B₆ Content (in milligrams) |
|------|-----------------------------------|
| Cow's Milk | 65-73 |
| Eggs | 22 |
| Corn | 250-570 |
| Oats | 190-250 |
| Whole Wheat | 270-410 |
| Wheat Germ | 1030-1120 |
| Peanuts | 300 |
| Split Peas | 190-400 |
| Cabbage | 290 |
| Potatoes | 160 |
| Bananas | 300 |
| Spinach | 83 |
| Dried Brewer's Yeast | 3930 |

### Minimum Daily Requirement

The recommended allowance for this vitamin for an average adult lies between 1500 and 2000 micrograms daily.

### Deficiencies

Deficiencies in Vitamin B₆ can lead to mental depression, sore mouth, lips and tongue, insomnia, nervousness, dizziness, nausea, and eczema.

## 5. *VITAMIN B₁₂ (CYANOCOBALAMIN)*

### Functions

— Necessary for normal growth and blood formation
— Maintains healthy nervous tissue
— Improves the biological value of vegetable proteins
— Prevents anemia

### Nonflesh Sources

Brewer's yeast, soybean milk, wheat germ, sea kelp, eggs and dairy products.

### Minimum Daily Requirements

There is a definite need in human nutrition for this vitamin, but no official minimum daily requirement has yet been established. A suggested MDR is between 3 and 5 micrograms.

### Deficiency

Can lead to pernicious anemia.
*Note:* It has been found that vegetarians who abstain from eggs and dairy products must be especially careful that they obtain adequate Vitamin $B_{12}$.

## C. *VITAMIN C (ASCORBIC ACID)* - Water Soluble

### *Functions*

— Promotes general nutrition
— Prevents scurvy, hemorrhaging, and diseases of the mouth and gums
— Aids in the absorption of iron in the intestinal tract
— Helps prevent colds

### *Sources*

Citrus fruits, acerola berries, rose hips, green peppers, tomatoes, broccoli, Brussels sprouts, strawberries, raw cabbage, turnip greens.

*Note:* Vitamin C is destroyed by drying and cooking. However, less destruction is caused in acid containing foods such as tomatoes.

### Table 11-14

**ASCORBIC ACID CONTENT IN FOODS, 100 grams edible portion**[30]

| Food | Ascorbic Acid Content (in milligrams) |
|---|---|
| Navel Oranges | 61 |
| Lemons | 53 |
| Grapefruit | 38 |
| Tangerines | 31 |
| Green Peppers, raw | 128 |
| Tomatoes, raw | 23 |
| Broccoli | 90 |
| Strawberries, raw | 59 |
| Brussels Sprouts | 87 |
| Turnip Greens, cooked | 69 |
| Acerola Berries | 1,300 |

### *Minimum Daily Requirements*

The minimum daily requirements for Vitamin C has been set at 60 milligrams for adult male, and 55 milligrams for an adult female.

### *Deficiencies*

Scurvy, sores in the mouth, anemia, softening of bones and teeth.

## D. *VITAMIN D* — (Fat Soluble)

### Functions

- Promotes normal calcification of bones (bone formation)
- Is important in the development of young people, and is needed by expectant mothers

### Sources

Direct sunlight, eggs, milk, butter.

### Minimum Daily Requirements

The suggested MDR is 100-250 International Units for adults and 400 International Units for children and adolescents.

### Deficiency

Can lead to rickets.

# E. *VITAMIN E* (Fat Soluble)

## *Functions*

- Serves as an antioxident, which is necessary for the formation of the nucleus of each body cell
- Prevents unsaturated fatty acids and fat-like substances from being destroyed in the body by oxygen
- Protects the body's store of vitamin A and C
- Aids in the well-being of the heart and general circulation
- Helps maintain healthy muscles

## *Principal Sources*

Unrefined vegetable oils, wheat germ, whole grain breads and cereals, legumes, green leaves, eggs, butter, margarine.

Table 11-15

**FOODS CONTAINING THE LARGEST AMOUNTS OF VITAMIN E**[81]

| Food | Milligrams of Vitamin E |
|---|---|
| Apples | .74 in 1 medium apple |
| Bacon | .53 in about 10 slices, broiled |
| Bananas | .40 in 1 medium banana |
| Navy Beans, dry | 3.60 in ½ cup, steamed |
| Beef Steak | .63 in 1 piece steak |
| Butter | 2.40 in 6 tablespoons |
| Carrots | .45 in 1 cup |
| Celery | .49 in 1 cup |
| Cornmeal, yellow | 1.70 in about ½ cup |
| Corn Oil | 87.00 in about 6 tablespoons |
| Eggs, whole | 1.00 in 1 whole egg |
| Grapefruit | .52 in about ½ grapefruit |
| Lettuce | .50 in 6 large leaves |
| Oatmeal | 2.10 in about ½ cup cooked oatmeal |
| Peas, Green | 2.10 in 1 cup peas |
| Potatoes, Sweet | 4.00 in one small potato |
| Rice, Brown | 2.40 in about ¾ cup cooked |
| Soybean Oil | 140.00 in 6 tablespoons |
| Turnip Greens | 2.30 in ½ cup steamed |
| Wheat Germ Oil, medicinal | 320.00 in 6 tablespoons |

## Minimum Daily Requirement

The daily need for vitamin E in adults is suggested to lie between 10 and 30 milligrams.

## Deficiencies

Deficiencies of Vitamin E can bring about the loss of pigmentation in the skin. Lack of sufficient Vitamin E has also been found to be a major cause of premature births.

## F. *VITAMIN K* (Fat Soluble)

### Function

Vitamin K is primarily essential for the clotting of blood.

### Sources

Green and yellow vegetables (especially dark leafy green ones), fruits, tubers, seeds, alfalfa, tomatoes, egg yolk, soybean oil.

### Minimum Daily Requirements

"A daily allowance for Vitamin K cannot be established because of the wide but inconsistent distribution of the Vitamin in the diet, and the variability of intestinal flora and absorption activity from person to person."[32]

### Deficiency

Although a deficiency of Vitamin K is unlikely to occur, insufficient amounts result in deficiencies in blood clotting.

### References

[1]Shelton, Herbert; *Health for the Millions*; Natural Hygiene Press, Chicago, 1968, p. 13
[2]*Ibid.*, p. 15
[3]Winter, Ruth; *Poisons in Your Food*; Crown Publishers Inc., New York, 1969, p. 5
[4]Taylor, C. M. and Pye, O. F.; *Foundations of Nutrition*; The Macmillan Company, New York, 1966, p. 115
[5]Orr, M. L. and Watt, B. K.; *Amino Acid Content of Foods*; United States Department of Agriculture, Washington, D.C., 1968, pp. 54-55

[6]Rose, W. C.; "The Amino Acid Requirements of Adult Man," *Nutrition Abstract and Review*, No. 27, 1957, p. 631

[7]Leverton, R. and Albanese, A. A., ed.; *Protein and Amino Acid Nutrition*; Academic Press, New York, 1959, p. 477

[8]*Review and Herald*; February 27, 1969, p. 3

[9]Watt, B. K. and Merrill, A. L.; *Composition of Foods;* United States Department of Agriculture, Washington, D.C., 1963, pp. 6-67

[10]Fredericks, Carleton and Baily, Herbert; *Food Facts and Fallacies*; The Julian Press, New York, 1965, p. 310

[11]Guthrie, Helen Andrews; *Introductory Nutrition;* The C. V. Mosby Co., St. Louis, 1967, p. 30

[12]Rodale, J. I. *et al.*; *Prevention Method for Better Health*; Rodale Books Inc., Emmaus, Pa., 1960, pp. 334-5

[13]Proudfit, F. T. and Robinson, C. H.; *Proudfit-Robinson's Normal and Therapeutic Nutrition*; 13th ed., The Macmillan Company, New York, 1967, p. 611

[14]*Ibid.*, p. 614

[15]Bieler, Henry G.; *Food is Your Best Medicine*; Random House, New York, 1965, p. 118

[16]*Ibid.*

[17]*Composition of Foods*; *op. cit.*, pp. 122-145

[18]*Introductory Nutrition*; *op. cit.*, p. 30

[19]*Composition of Foods*; *op. cit.*, pp. 6-67

[20]*Ibid.*

[21]*Ibid.*

[22]*Ibid.*

[23]*Foundations of Nutrition*; *op. cit.*, p. 155

[24]*Ibid.*, p. 289

[25]*Composition of Foods*; *op. cit.*

[26]*Ibid.*

[27]*Ibid.*

[28]*Ibid.*

[29]*Foundations of Nutrition*; *op. cit.*, p. 289

[30]*Composition of Foods*; *op. cit.*

[31]Rodale, J. I. *et al.*; *The Complete Book of Vitamins*; Rodale Books Inc., Emmaus, Pa., 1966, p. 349

[32]*Foundations of Nutrition*; *op. cit.*, p. 286

Note: For Additional Sources, See Appendix G.

# Appendices

# APPENDIX A

# WHAT TO EAT IF YOU DON'T EAT MEAT

(some high protein suggestions)

BEANS AND OTHER LEGUMES: Soybeans, lentils, garbanzos, navy beans, limas, split peas, bean sprouts. Can be used in soups, casseroles, salads, loaves, dips, and sauces.

GRAINS AND CEREALS: Wheat and wheat germ, rolled oats, rice, millet, corn. Especially good for pancakes and waffles, grits, mush, oatmeal, wholegrain breads, and dinner loaves. When combined with animal or soybean milk, grains and cereal products provide a very good combination of proteins.

DAIRY PRODUCTS: Eggs, milk, buttermilk, sour cream, cheese (cottage, cream, cheddar), yogurt, ice cream. Recipes using these foods include omelettes (cheese, herb, mushroom, onion, jelly), quiche Lorraine, soufflés (cheese, spinach, chocolate), soups (cream of mushroom, potato, asparagus), breads and pastry, Welsh rarebit, macaroni and cheese, cheese or egg salad sandwiches, cheese sauce for vegetables, cheese blintzes, pizza, cheese and eggs in salads or alone. Dairy products also enhance the nutritional value of casseroles, dinner loaves, and sauces.

TEXTURED SOYBEAN AND WHEAT PROTEINS: High protein commercially processed vegetable products prepared as substitutes for such meat products as loaves, burgers, franks, steak, chicken, ham, bacon, and turkey. Can be used in place of meat in main dishes, or in soups, salads, and appetizers.

NUTS AND SEEDS: Almonds, pecans, walnuts, Brazil nuts, filberts, cashews, peanuts; sesame, sunflower and pumpkin seeds; pine nuts (piñón). Can be eaten cooked or raw and combined with fruits and vegetables in salads, or cooked in loaves, casseroles, breads, soups, and cereals. Nuts and seeds are delicious when eaten raw by themselves.

## APPENDIX B

## SELECTED VEGETARIAN RECIPES

### Crunchy Granola

7½ c. rolled oats
1 c. wheat germ
1½ tsp. sea salt
½ c. ground raw nuts
½ c. vegetable oil

½ c. honey
½ c. sesame seeds
1½ c. shredded coconut
1/3 c. hot water

Mix ingredients together. Spread the mixture across bottom of large baking sheet or pan. Bake at 350°, for about 35 minutes, or until granola turns golden brown. Stir twice so that everything toasts evenly. Serves 4 people for a week.

### Hearty Vegetarian Vegetable Soup

2 medium onions,
    chopped
3 stalks celery
2 tbs. vegetable oil or
    margarine
2 qts. water
4 tbs. vegetable base
3 med. tomatoes, cubed

2 lg. potatoes, cubed
2 lg. carrots, diced
6 med. mushrooms
¼ c. parsley
Peas, corn, beans
¼ c. barley
¼ c. brown rice

Brown the onions and celery in oil; then add water, vegetables, and the other ingredients. Season to taste. Cook until it is to your liking.

### Ahimsa Pea Soup

2 qts. water
2 c. split peas
2 carrots, diced

2 stalks celery, diced
2 onions, cubed
¼ c. vegetable base

Boil the mixture until peas are soft. Season to taste.

## Potato Mushroom Soup

2 med. onions, cubed
6 stalks celery, diced
2 lg. potatoes, cubed

½ lb. mushrooms, sliced
1 c. milk (cow's or
soybean)

Boil mixture until potatoes are soft. Season to taste. Then add the milk. Soups serve 6 hungry people.

## Stuffed Peppers

4 lg. green peppers
1 med. onion, chopped
2 tbs. olive oil
½ c. brown rice
1½ c. water
1 tsp. salt
1 tsp. basil

1 tsp. ground black
pepper
1 bay leaf
2 tsp. parsley
½ c. almonds, chopped
Tomato sauce
Wheat germ

Cook the brown rice in water, to which the mixed spices have been added. Cooking time should be about 45 minutes. Cut off tops of peppers, seed, and parboil. Set aside. Mix rice mixture with ground almonds. Place peppers in casserole; fill with rice-almond mixture. Sprinkle with wheat germ and cover with tomato sauce. Bake for ½ hour at moderate heat (350°). Serves 4.

## Soybean Burgers

2 c. soybeans, soaked
(overnight) and
cooked.
1 small onion, chopped
¾ c. wheat germ

1 carrot, grated
½ tsp. salt
3 tbs. parsley
½ tsp. ground dill
2 eggs.

Mix all ingredients together, and form into patties. Fry in a small amount of vegetable oil until golden brown. Serves 6.

## Kasha (Buckwheat Groats)

2 c. boiling water      ½ tsp. salt
1 c. kasha            1 egg (optional)

Cook until kasha is soft (10-15 minutes), adding egg before kasha is placed in water.

4 onions, sliced.        ½ c. sunflower seeds (or
½ lb. mushrooms, sliced    other seeds)
2 tsp. oil

Brown the onions in the oil, then add mushrooms and seeds. Combine with the kasha, and serve. Serves 4.

## Walnut-Almond Loaf

1 c. walnuts, ground     ¼ c. wheat germ
1 c. almonds, ground     ¼ c. parsley or chervil
½ c. soybean grits, soak-  1 tsp. salt
    ed in 1 c. vegetable   1 tsp. pepper
    broth              ½ c. cooked brown rice
3 eggs

Mix all the ingredients together. Mixture should be slightly moist—if necessary, add more liquid or dry ingredients whatever the case may be. Bake in oiled loaf pan for ½ hour at 350°. Serve hot with tomato or cheese sauce.

## Colombian Spinach Bake

1 pkg. chopped spinach,   ½ cup grated cheddar
    fresh or frozen         cheese
Few pinches of salt      Wheat germ or bread
1 c. sour cream           crumbs
                        Margarine or butter

Cook spinach as directed on package and drain *thoroughly!* Add the salt and sour cream. Place in greased 1 quart casserole. Sprinkle with the cheese, and the wheat germ or crumbs. Dot with pats of butter or margarine. Bake for ½ hour in a 350° oven. Serves 6.

## Eggplant Medley

1 lg. onion, sliced
1 med. eggplant, cubed
½ lb. zucchini
½ lb. mushrooms
1 lg. pepper

2 tbs. vegetable oil or
    margarine
Sm. can tomato sauce
Parsley, salt, pepper

Sauté the eggplant and onions in oil in a large frypan until slightly soft. Add the mushrooms, zucchini, and pepper, and cook for several minutes. Add the tomato sauce, and flavor to taste. Heat for another minute or so and serve. Serves 2.

## Lentils & Rice Unité

2 cups lentils
1 cup brown rice
1 med. onion

1 tbs. butter or margarine
1 tbs. chopped parsley
2 tsp. salt

Wash and soak the lentils overnight, drain. Cover the lentils with boiling water and boil for two hours, adding 1 tsp. salt (or other seasoning). Cook the rice as you would usually. Fry the onion carefully in pan, just enough so that it's cooked through. Place the lentils in center of a large platter, pour the onions over the lentils, and place the rice around the lentils. Sprinkle with parsley or whatever. Serves 4.

## Golden Chicken Bake

4 cups sliced soymeat
    (fried chicken style)
2 tbsp. butter

1 tbsp. minced parsley
1 can condensed mush-
    room soup

Arrange sliced soymeat in single layer in shallow baking dish. Dribble melted butter over it. Stir soup, pour over soymeat; sprinkle parsley on top. Bake 20 minutes at 400 degrees F.

## Millet-Nut Loaf

1/3 cup hulled sunflower
seeds, finely chopped
or soak for half hour
1/3 cup sesame seed meal
1/3 cup walnuts or al-
monds or pecans,
finely chopped
3 eggs, lightly beaten
1½ tbsp. melted butter
or cooking oil
1½ cups milk
Dash paprika
1½ cups cooked lima

beans, mashed or
green peas
1½ cups cooked carrots,
chopped
2 tbsp. minced onion or
chives
1½ cups soft cooked
millet
Salt to taste
2 tsp. lemon juice
1½ cups American
cheese, grated

Add the milk and lightly beaten eggs to the millet and
combine all ingredients. Pack into a well greased loaf
pan. Bake in moderate oven 350 degrees F for 45 minutes,
or until firm. Serve with tomato, cream or mushroom
sauce.

## Cottage Cheese Pie

2 cups cottage cheese
1 cup each diced cooked
carrots, potatoes,
celery, onions
1 cup cooked peas
1 cup fine noodles,
cooked and drained

½ cup melted butter
1 tbsp. seasoning broth
Liquids from cooked
vegetables
Biscuit dough

Combine cottage cheese, vegetables, noodles and broth.
Make thin gravy from broth and vegetable juices. Fill individual casseroles ¾ full of vegetables and cottage cheese
mixture. Cover with gravy and place small round biscuit
dough over top. Large casserole may be used if desired,
and mixture covered with pastry crust. Place in moderate
oven, 350 degrees F and bake until biscuits are done.

## Cheese Blintzes

Crepes:

| | |
|---|---|
| ½ c. cold water | 2 eggs, beaten |
| ½ c. cold milk | Salt |
| 2 tsp. melted butter or margarine | 1 c. flour |

Mix water, milk, and eggs. Add the salt, flour, and melted butter. Mix in a blender for 1 minute, and then place in refrigerator for at least 2 hours.

Heat crepe pan (8″ omelette pan), and brush with butter. Place tablespoon of batter on pan and rotate pan to spread the batter. Cook until no longer shiny and turn out onto clean dish towel. Repeat until all the batter is used up.

Stuffing:

| | |
|---|---|
| 1 lb. dry cottage cheese (pot cheese type) | ½ c. sugar |
| | ½ c. raisins |
| 1 egg | 1 tsp. cinnamon |

Mix contents well. Place tablespoonful on each crepe and roll securely. Sauté blintzes in large frypan until light brown. Serve with sour cream and applesauce. 3 or 4 blintzes per person. Serves 6.

## APPENDIX C

## VEGETARIANISM IN LITERATURE

Whenever I see a meat and fish-ridden dining table I know that I am looking upon one of the seeds of war and hatred. . . There is war where there is misery anywhere, where there is discontent and unhappiness. Every one of us is responsible for the misery of the poor and helplessness of the weak, for the helplessness of the average animal. The animal that can be killed for food. He can be mutilated in the vivisection chamber for our benefit. He can be beaten and not a word will go forth on his behalf. When people ask me, "Is there likely to be a future war?" I answer "Yes, until the animals are treated as our younger brothers."

—Dr. George S. Arundale
*Conscience,* 1939-45

World peace, or any other kind of peace, depends greatly on the attitude of the mind. Vegetarianism can bring about the right mental attitude for peace. In this world of lusts and hatreds, greed and anger, force and violence, vegetarianism holds forth a way of life, which if practised universally, can lead to a better, juster and more peaceful community of nations.

—U Nu, Former Prime Minister of Burma
*The Vegetarian Way;* Special Number, XIX World Vegetarian Congress — 1967

The demand for vegetarian food will increase our production for the right kind of plant foods. We shall cease to breed pigs and other animals for food, thereby ceasing to be responsible for the horror of slaughterhouses where millions of creatures cry in agony and in vain because of man's selfishness. If such concentration camps for suffering continue, can peace ever come to earth? Can we escape the responsibility for misery when we are practising killing every day of our lives by consciously or unconsciously supporting this trade of slaughter? Peace cannot come where Peace is not given.

—Rukmini Devi Arundale
*The Vegetarian Way,* Special Number, XIX World Vegetarian Congress — 1967

I do not see any reason why animals should be slaughtered to serve as human diet when there are so many substitutes. After all, man can live without meat. It is only some carnivorous animals that have to subsist on flesh. Killing animals for sport, for pleasure, for adventures, and for hides and furs is a phenomenon which is at once disgusting and distressing. There is no justification in indulging in such acts of brutality.

—H. H. The Dalai Lama of Tibet
*The Vegetarian Way,* Special Number, XIX World Vegetarian Congress — 1967

If animals could talk, would we then dare to kill and eat them? How could we then justify such fratricide?

—Francois Voltaire
*Princes of Babylon*

. . . It is my view that the Vegetarian manner of living by its purely physical effect on the human temperament would most beneficially influence the lot of mankind.

—Albert Einstein
Letter to *Vegetarian Watch-Tower* December 27, 1930

It is only by softening and disguising dead flesh by culinary preparation that it is rendered susceptible of mastication or digestion, and that the sight of its bloody juices and raw horror does not excite loathing and disgust.

> —Percy Bysshe Shelley
> *Vindication of a Natural Diet*
> Albuquerque; University of New Mexico Press, 1954

At the same instant the ear was assailed by a most terrifying shriek; the visitors started in alarm, the women turned pale and shrank back. The shriek was followed by another, louder and yet more agonizing—for once started upon that journey, the hog never came back; at the top of the wheel he was shunted off upon a trolley, and went sailing down the room. And meantime another was swung up, and then another, and another, until there was a double line of them, each dangling by a foot and kicking in frenzy—and squealing. The uproar was appalling, perilous to the ear-drums; one feared there was too much sound for the room to hold—that the walls must give way or the ceiling crack. There were high squeals and low squeals, grunts, and wails of agony; there would come a momentary lull, and then a fresh outburst, louder than ever, surging up to a deafening climax. It was too much for some of the visitors—the men would look at each other, laughing nervously, and the women would stand with hands clenched and the blood rushing to their faces, and the tears starting in their eyes.

> —Upton Sinclair
> *The Jungle*; Boston, Robert Bentley, Inc., 1971, p. 35

Forbear, O mortals,
To spoil your bodies with such impious food!
There is corn for you, apples, whose weight bears down
The bending branches; there are grapes that swell

On the green vines, and pleasant herbs, and greens
Made mellow and soft with cooking; there is milk
And clover-honey. Earth is generous
With her provision, and her sustenance
Is very kind; she offers, for your tables,
Food that requires no bloodshed and no slaughter.

> —Ovid
> *Metamorphoses*; Bloomington, Indiana University
> Press, 1958, pp. 367-8

In all the round world of Utopia there is no meat. There used to be. But now we cannot stand the thought of slaughterhouses. And, in a population that is all educated, and at about the same level of physical refinement, it is practically impossible to find anyone who will hew a dead ox or pig. We never settled the hygienic question of meat-eating at all. This other aspect decided us. I can still remember, as a boy, the rejoicings over the closing of the last slaughterhouse.

> —H. G. Wells
> *A Modern Utopia*; Lincoln, University of Nebraska
> Press, 1967, p. 286

Who finds the heifer dead and bleeding fresh
And sees fast by a butcher with an ax,
Who will suspect 'twas he that made the slaughter?

> —William Shakespeare
> *King Henry VI* (second part) ; Act III, Scene II,
> lines 188-90)

I am the voice of the voiceless
Through me the dumb shall speak
Til' the deaf world's ear shall be made to hear
The wrongs of the wordless weak.
The same force formed the sparrow
That fashioned man, the king.

The God of the whole gave a spark of soul
To furred and feathered thing;
And I am my brother's keeper,
And I will fight his fight.
And speak the word for beast and bird
Till the world shall set things right.

—Ella Wheeler Wilcox

## SONG OF PEACE

We are the living graves of murdered beasts,
Slaughtered to satisfy our appetites,
We never pause to wonder at our feasts,
If animals, like men, can possibly have rights.
We pray on Sundays that we may have light,
To guide our foot-steps on the paths we tread.
We're sick of war, we do not want to fight,
The thought of it now fills our hearts with dread
And yet we gorge ourselves upon the dead.
Like carrion crows, we live and feed on meat,
Regardless of the suffering and pain
We cause by doing so. If thus we treat
Defenceless animals for sport or gain,
How can we hope in this world to attain
The PEACE we say we are so anxious for?
We pray for it, o'er hecatombs of slain,
To God, while outraging the moral law,
Thus cruelty begets its offspring—War.

—George Bernard Shaw

He who permits (the slaughter of an animal), he who cuts it up, he who kills it, he who buys or sells (meat), he who cooks it, he who serves it up, and he who eats it (must all be considered as) the slayers (of the animal).

—*The Laws of Manu,* V. 51; p. 176
Motilal Banarsidass; Delhi, 1967

# APPENDIX D
# VEGANISM?

A vegan is one who is a pure vegetarian, whose food includes fruits, nuts, vegetables, and grains. All animal food is excluded from the vegan diet, such as milk, cheese, eggs, and honey. The vegan philosophy is based largely on health, ecological, and moral grounds.

## Health

Vegans maintain that dairy products are not "natural food" for man, and therefore should be avoided. In addition, it has been found that a vegan diet is lower in cholesterol and in pesticide/hormone residues than both the lacto-ovo-vegetarian and nonvegetarian regimens.

## Ecology

According to Dr. Aaron Altschul of the U.S.D.A., the pure vegetable diet uses much less land and only 1/7 of the water as a mixed animal and vegetable diet.

## Moral

Many vegans maintain that although the taking of dairy products entails no killing, the animals are exploited and later killed when their production slackens. In addition, it is cited that the use of dairy products involves the slaughter of bull calves, making the consumer indirectly responsible for the slaughter. Vegans also generally abstain from other animal products as well, which include leather, wool, fur, honey, and any other product involving the exploitation of animal life by man.

## Is a Vegan Diet Safe?

It is generally felt that a well chosen pure vegetarian diet is more than adequate to ensure good health. However, some nutritionists suggest a daily supplement of Vitamin $B_{12}$ for those who choose a vegan diet.

# APPENDIX E

## SOME LIVESTOCK BY-PRODUCTS AND THEIR USES

Sources: American Meat Institute; Chicago, Illinois.
The Meat Packers Council of Canada; Islington, Ontario.

### Gelatin

Confectionary
Marshmallow
Ice Cream
Gelatin Desserts
Pharmaceutical Products

### Hide

Shoes, Wearing Apparel
Upholstery
Luggage
Glue
Fertilizer

### Hair

Brushes
Rug Pads
Upholstering Material

### Blood

Livestock Feeds
Pharmaceuticals

## Fats

Lard
Shortening
Soaps
Cosmetics
Animal Feeds
Chewing Gum

## Glands

Insulin
A.C.T.H.
Adrenalin

## Intestines & Catgut

Sausage Casings
Music Strings
Tennis Racket Strings

## Bones, Horns, Hooves

Buttons
Glue
Used in Sugar Refining
Livestock Feeds
Fertilizer

# APPENDIX F

# APPENDIX F
# FOOD VALUES

(After *Nutritive Value of Foods*, Home and Garden Bulletin No. 72, United States Department of Agriculture, Washington, D. C.)

| FOOD | MEASURE | WEIGHT grams | FOOD ENERGY Calories | PROTEIN grams | FAT grams | CALCIUM milligrams | IRON milligrams | VITAMIN A Int'l Units | VITAMIN B₁ milligrams | VITAMIN B₂ milligrams | VITAMIN B₃ milligrams | VITAMIN C milligrams |
|---|---|---|---|---|---|---|---|---|---|---|---|---|
| **DAIRY PRODUCTS** | | | | | | | | | | | | |
| *MILK* | | | | | | | | | | | | |
| Cow's milk (whole fluid) | 1 cup | 244 | 160 | 9 | 9 | 288 | 0.1 | 350 | 0.07 | 0.41 | 0.2 | 2 |
| Cow's milk (nonfat, dry) | 1 cup | 104 | 375 | 37 | 1 | 1,345 | .6 | 30 | .36 | 1.85 | .9 | 7 |
| Soybean powder (low fat, dry) (for comparison) | 1 cup | 100 | 250 | 52 | 5.6 | 244 | 13.0 | 70 | 1.10 | .35 | 2.9 | — |
| *CHEESE* | | | | | | | | | | | | |
| Cheddar cheese | 1 oz | 28 | 115 | 7 | 9 | 213 | .3 | 370 | .01 | .13 | trace | 0 |
| Cottage cheese (creamed, curd pressed down) | 1 cup | 245 | 260 | 33 | 10 | 230 | .7 | 420 | .07 | .61 | .2 | 0 |
| Processed cheese, American | 1 oz. | 28 | 105 | 7 | 9 | 198 | .3 | 350 | .01 | .12 | trace | 0 |
| *CREAM* | | | | | | | | | | | | |
| Half and half | 1 cup | 242 | 325 | 8 | 28 | 261 | .1 | 1,160 | .07 | .39 | .1 | 2 |
| Ice cream (10% fat) | 1 cup | 133 | 255 | 6 | 14 | 194 | .1 | 590 | .05 | .28 | .1 | 1 |

| | Measure | | | | | | | | | | | |
|---|---|---|---|---|---|---|---|---|---|---|---|---|
| ***EGGS*** | | | | | | | | | | | | |
| Eggs, large, whole | 1 egg | 50 | 80 | 6 | 6 | 27 | 1.1 | 590 | .05 | .15 | trace | 0 |
| **MEAT, POULTRY, FISH** | | | | | | | | | | | | |
| ***MEAT*** | | | | | | | | | | | | |
| Beef, ground, broiled | 3 oz | 85 | 245 | 21 | 17 | 9 | 2.7 | 30 | .07 | .18 | 4.6 | — |
| Beefsteak, Sirloin, broiled | 3 oz | 85 | 330 | 20 | 27 | 9 | 2.5 | 50 | .05 | .16 | 4.0 | — |
| Frankfurter, heated | 1 frank | 56 | 170 | 7 | 15 | 3 | .8 | — | .08 | .11 | 1.4 | — |
| Porkchops, cooked, with bone | 3.5 oz. | 98 | 260 | 16 | 21 | 8 | 2.2 | 0 | .63 | .18 | 3.8 | — |
| Veal Cutlet, cooked, w/out bone | 3 oz | 85 | 185 | 23 | 9 | 9 | 2.7 | — | .06 | .21 | 4.6 | — |
| ***POULTRY*** | | | | | | | | | | | | |
| Chicken, flesh only, broiled | 3 oz | 85 | 115 | 20 | 3 | 8 | 1.4 | 80 | .05 | .16 | 7.4 | — |
| ***FISH*** | | | | | | | | | | | | |
| Haddock, breaded, fried | 3 oz | 85 | 140 | 17 | 5 | 34 | 1.0 | — | .03 | .06 | 2.7 | 2 |
| Tuna, canned in oil, drained | 3 oz | 85 | 170 | 24 | 7 | 7 | 1.6 | 70 | .04 | .10 | 10.1 | — |
| **DRY BEANS, PEAS, NUTS** | | | | | | | | | | | | |
| Almonds, shelled, whole | 1 cup | 142 | 850 | 26 | 77 | 332 | 6.7 | 0 | .34 | 1.31 | 5.0 | trace |
| Beans, Great Northern, cooked, drained | 1 cup | 180 | 210 | 14 | 1 | 90 | 4.9 | 0 | .25 | .13 | 1.3 | 0 |
| Beans, Lima, cooked, drained | 1 cup | 190 | 260 | 16 | 1 | 55 | 5.9 | 0 | .25 | .11 | 1.3 | 0 |
| Beans, Navy, cooked, drained | 1 cup | 190 | 225 | 15 | 1 | 95 | 5.1 | 0 | .27 | .13 | 1.3 | 0 |
| Cashews, roasted | 1 cup | 140 | 785 | 24 | 64 | 53 | 5.3 | 140 | .60 | .35 | 2.5 | — |
| Coconut, fresh, shredded | 1 cup | 130 | 450 | 5 | 46 | 17 | 2.2 | 0 | .07 | .03 | .7 | 4 |
| Cowpeas, cooked, drained | 1 cup | 248 | 190 | 13 | 1 | 42 | 3.2 | 20 | .41 | .11 | 1.1 | trace |
| [2]Lentils, dry, cooked | 1 cup | 250 | 265 | 20 | trace | 68 | 5.3 | 150 | .93 | .55 | 5.0 | 0 |
| Peanuts, roasted, halves | 1 cup | 144 | 840 | 37 | 72 | 107 | 3.0 | — | .46 | .19 | 24.7 | 0 |
| Peanut butter | 1 tbsp. | 16 | 95 | 4 | 8 | 9 | .3 | — | .02 | .02 | 2.4 | — |
| Peas, split, dry, cooked | 1 cup | 250 | 290 | 20 | 1 | 28 | 4.2 | 100 | .37 | .22 | 2.2 | 2 |
| Pecans, halves | 1 cup | 108 | 740 | 10 | 77 | 79 | 2.6 | 140 | .93 | .14 | 1.0 | 0 |
| [3]Soybeans, dry, cooked | 1 cup | 180 | 208 | 18 | 9 | 117 | 4.3 | 48 | .34 | .14 | 1.0 | — |
| Walnuts, black, chopped | 1 cup | 126 | 790 | 26 | 75 | trace | 7.6 | 380 | .28 | .14 | .9 | — |

## VEGETABLES

| FOOD | MEASURE | WEIGHT grams | FOOD ENERGY Calories | PROTEIN grams | FAT grams | CALCIUM milligrams | IRON milligrams | VITAMIN A Int'l Units | VITAMIN B₁ milligrams | VITAMIN B₂ milligrams | VITAMIN B₂ milligrams | VITAMIN C milligrams |
|---|---|---|---|---|---|---|---|---|---|---|---|---|
| Asparagus, cooked, drained, pieces | 1 cup | 145 | 30 | 3 | trace | 30 | .9 | 1,310 | .23 | .26 | 2.0 | 38 |
| Beans, green, cooked, drained | 1 cup | 125 | 30 | 2 | trace | 63 | .8 | 680 | .09 | .11 | .6 | 15 |
| Bean sprouts, mung, cooked, drained | 1 cup | 125 | 35 | 4 | trace | 21 | 1.1 | 30 | .11 | .13 | .9 | 8 |
| Beets, cooked, drained, sliced | 1 cup | 170 | 55 | 2 | trace | 24 | .9 | 30 | .05 | .07 | .5 | 10 |
| Beet greens, cooked, drained | 1 cup | 145 | 25 | 3 | trace | 144 | 2.8 | 7,400 | .10 | .22 | .4 | 22 |
| Broccoli, cooked, drained | 1 cup | 155 | 40 | 5 | 1 | 136 | 1.2 | 3,880 | .14 | .31 | 1.2 | 140 |
| Brussels sprouts, cooked | 1 cup | 155 | 55 | 7 | 1 | 50 | 1.7 | 810 | .12 | .22 | 1.2 | 135 |
| Cabbage, raw, (coarsely shredded) | 1 cup | 70 | 15 | 1 | trace | 34 | .3 | 90 | .04 | .04 | .2 | 33 |
| Carrots, raw (5½ x 1 inch) | 1 carrot | 50 | 20 | 1 | trace | 18 | .4 | 5,500 | .03 | .03 | .3 | 4 |
| Cauliflower, cooked, flowerbuds | 1 cup | 120 | 25 | 3 | trace | 25 | .8 | 70 | .11 | .10 | .7 | 66 |
| Celery, large stalk (8x1½ in.) | 1 stalk | 40 | 5 | trace | trace | 16 | .1 | 100 | .01 | .01 | .1 | 4 |
| Corn, sweet, ear (5x1¾ in.), cooked | 1 ear | 140 | 70 | 3 | 1 | 2 | .5 | 310 | .09 | .08 | 1.0 | 7 |
| Cucumbers, raw, pared (7½x2 in.) | 1 cucumber | 207 | 30 | 1 | trace | 35 | .6 | trace | .07 | .09 | .4 | 23 |
| Dandelion greens, cooked | 1 cup | 180 | 60 | 4 | 1 | 252 | 3.2 | 21,060 | .24 | .29 | — | 32 |
| Kale, stems, leaves, cooked | 1 cup | 110 | 30 | 4 | 1 | 147 | 1.3 | 8,140 | — | — | — | 68 |
| Lettuce, Iceberg (4¾ in diam.) | 1 head | 454 | 60 | 4 | trace | 91 | 2.3 | 1,500 | .29 | .27 | 1.3 | 29 |
| Mustard greens, cooked | 1 cup | 140 | 35 | 3 | 1 | 193 | 2.5 | 8,120 | .11 | .19 | .9 | 68 |
| Onions, raw (2½ in. diam.) | 1 onion | 110 | 40 | 2 | trace | 30 | .6 | 40 | .04 | .04 | .2 | 11 |

| Food | Measure | Grams | Calories | Protein (g) | Fat (g) | Calcium (mg) | Iron (mg) | Vitamin A (I.U.) | Thiamine (mg) | Riboflavin (mg) | Niacin (mg) | Ascorbic Acid (mg) |
|---|---|---|---|---|---|---|---|---|---|---|---|---|
| Parsley, raw, chopped | 1 tbsp | 4 | trace | trace | trace | 8 | .2 | 340 | trace | .01 | trace | 7 |
| Parsnips, cooked | 1 cup | 155 | 100 | 2 | 1 | 70 | .9 | 50 | .11 | .12 | .2 | 16 |
| Peas, green, cooked | 1 cup | 160 | 115 | 9 | 1 | 37 | 2.9 | 860 | .44 | .17 | 3.7 | 33 |
| Peppers, sweet, raw, medium | 1 pod | 74 | 15 | 1 | trace | 7 | .5 | 310 | .06 | .06 | .4 | 94 |
| Potatoes, baked, medium | 1 potato | 99 | 90 | 3 | trace | 9 | .7 | trace | .10 | .04 | 1.7 | 20 |
| Radishes, raw, small, w/out tops | 4 radishes | 40 | 5 | trace | trace | 12 | .4 | trace | .01 | .01 | .1 | 10 |
| Spinach, cooked | 1 cup | 180 | 40 | 5 | 1 | 167 | 4.0 | 14,580 | .13 | .25 | 1.0 | 50 |
| Squash, winter, baked | 1 cup | 205 | 130 | 4 | 1 | 57 | 1.6 | 8,610 | .10 | .27 | 1.4 | 27 |
| Sweet potatoes, (5x2 in.) baked | 1 sweet potato | 110 | 155 | 2 | 1 | 44 | 1.0 | 8,910 | .10 | .07 | .7 | 24 |
| Tomatoes, raw (3 in. diam.) | 1 tomato | 200 | 40 | 2 | trace | 24 | .9 | 1,640 | .11 | .07 | 1.3 | 42 |
| Tomato juice, canned | 1 cup | 243 | 45 | 2 | trace | 17 | 2.2 | 1,940 | .12 | .07 | 1.9 | 39 |
| Turnips, cooked, diced | 1 cup | 155 | 35 | 1 | trace | 54 | .6 | trace | .06 | .08 | .5 | 34 |
| Turnip greens, cooked | 1 cup | 145 | 30 | 3 | trace | 252 | 1.5 | 8,270 | .15 | .33 | .7 | 68 |
| **FRUITS and FRUIT PRODUCTS** | | | | | | | | | | | | |
| Apples, raw (3 per lb) | 1 apple | 150 | 70 | trace | trace | 8 | .4 | 50 | .04 | .02 | .1 | 3 |
| Apple juice, bottled or canned | 1 cup | 248 | 120 | trace | trace | 15 | 1.5 | — | .02 | .05 | .2 | 2 |
| Applesauce, canned, unsweetened | 1 cup | 244 | 100 | 1 | trace | 10 | 1.2 | 100 | .05 | .02 | .1 | 2 |
| Apricots, dried, uncooked | 1 cup | 150 | 390 | 8 | 1 | 100 | 8.2 | 16,350 | .02 | .23 | 4.9 | 19 |
| Apricot nectar, canned | 1 cup | 251 | 140 | 1 | trace | 23 | .5 | 2,380 | .03 | .03 | .5 | 8 |
| Avocados, California, raw (diam. 3⅛ inches) | 1 avocado | 284 | 370 | 5 | 37 | 22 | 1.3 | 630 | .24 | .43 | 3.5 | 30 |
| Bananas, raw, medium | 1 banana | 175 | 100 | 1 | trace | 10 | .8 | 230 | .06 | .07 | .8 | 12 |
| Blackberries, raw | 1 cup | 144 | 85 | 2 | 1 | 46 | 1.3 | 290 | .05 | .06 | .5 | 30 |
| Blueberries, raw | 1 cup | 140 | 85 | 1 | 1 | 21 | 1.4 | 140 | .04 | .08 | .6 | 20 |
| Cantaloups, raw, med. (5 inch diam.) | ½ melon | 385 | 60 | 1 | trace | 27 | .8 | 6,540 | .08 | .06 | 1.2 | 63 |
| Dates, pitted, cut | 1 cup | 178 | 490 | 4 | 1 | 105 | 5.3 | 90 | .16 | .17 | 3.9 | 0 |
| Figs, dried, large (2x1 inch) | 1 fig | 21 | 60 | 1 | trace | 26 | .6 | 20 | .02 | .02 | .1 | 0 |
| Grapefruit, raw, med. pink or red | ½ grapefruit | 241 | 50 | 1 | trace | 20 | .5 | 540 | .05 | .02 | .2 | 44 |

| FOOD | MEASURE | WEIGHT grams | FOOD ENERGY Calories | PROTEIN grams | FAT grams | CALCIUM milligrams | IRON milligrams | VITAMIN A Int'l Units | VITAMIN B₁ milligrams | VITAMIN B₂ milligrams | VITAMIN B₃ milligrams | VITAMIN C Milligrams |
|---|---|---|---|---|---|---|---|---|---|---|---|---|
| Grapefruit juice, canned, white, unsweetened) | 1 cup | 247 | 100 | 1 | trace | 20 | 1.0 | 20 | .07 | .04 | .4 | 84 |
| Grapes, raw, American Type | 1 cup | 153 | 65 | 1 | 1 | 15 | .4 | 100 | .05 | .03 | .2 | 3 |
| Lemons, raw (2⅛ in. diam.) | 1 lemon | 110 | 20 | 1 | trace | 19 | .4 | 10 | .03 | .01 | .1 | 39 |
| Olives, green, pickled | 4 med. | 16 | 15 | trace | 2 | 8 | .2 | 40 | — | — | — | — |
| Oranges, raw (2⅞ in. diam.) | 1 orange | 180 | 65 | 1 | trace | 54 | .5 | 260 | .13 | .05 | .5 | 66 |
| Orange juice, fresh | 1 cup | 248 | 110 | 2 | 1 | 27 | .5 | 500 | .22 | .07 | 1.0 | 124 |
| Papayas, raw, ½ inch cubes | 1 cup | 182 | 70 | 1 | trace | 36 | .5 | 3,190 | .07 | .08 | .5 | 102 |
| Peaches, raw, medium | 1 peach | 114 | 35 | 1 | trace | 9 | .5 | 1,320 | .02 | .05 | 1.0 | 7 |
| Pears, raw (3x2½ in. diam) | 1 pear | 182 | 100 | 1 | 1 | 13 | .5 | 30 | .04 | .07 | .2 | 7 |
| Pineapple, raw, diced | 1 cup | 140 | 75 | 1 | trace | 24 | .7 | 100 | .12 | .04 | .3 | 24 |
| Plums, raw (2 inch diam.) | 1 plum | 60 | 25 | trace | trace | 7 | .3 | 140 | .02 | .02 | .3 | 3 |
| Raisins, seedless, pressed down | 1 cup | 165 | 480 | 4 | trace | 102 | 5.8 | 30 | .18 | .13 | .8 | 2 |
| Raspberries, red, raw | 1 cup | 123 | 70 | 1 | 1 | 27 | 1.1 | 160 | .04 | .11 | 1.1 | 31 |
| Strawberries, raw, capped | 1 cup | 149 | 55 | 1 | 1 | 31 | 1.5 | 90 | .04 | .10 | 1.0 | 88 |
| Tangerines, raw, medium | 1 tangerine | 116 | 40 | 1 | trace | 34 | .3 | 360 | .05 | .02 | .1 | 27 |
| Watermelon, raw, 4x8 inch wedge | 1 wedge | 925 | 115 | 2 | 1 | 30 | 2.1 | 2,510 | .13 | .13 | .7 | 30 |

## SUGARS, SWEETS

| FOOD | MEASURE | WEIGHT grams | FOOD ENERGY Calories | PROTEIN grams | FAT grams | CALCIUM milligrams | IRON milligrams | VITAMIN A Int'l Units | VITAMIN B₁ milligrams | VITAMIN B₂ milligrams | VITAMIN B₃ milligrams | VITAMIN C Milligrams |
|---|---|---|---|---|---|---|---|---|---|---|---|---|
| Honey, strained or extracted | 1 tbsp | 21 | 65 | trace | 0 | 1 | .1 | 0 | trace | .01 | .1 | trace |
| Sugar, brown, firm packed | 1 cup | 220 | 280 | 0 | 0 | 187 | 7.5 | 0 | .02 | .07 | .4 | 0 |
| Sugar, white, granulated | 1 cup | 200 | 770 | 0 | 0 | 0 | .2 | 0 | 0 | 0 | 0 | 0 |

## GRAIN PRODUCTS

| Food | Measure | | | | | | | | | | | |
|---|---|---|---|---|---|---|---|---|---|---|---|---|
| Barley, pearled, light, uncooked | 1 cup | 200 | 700 | 16 | 2 | 32 | 4.0 | 0 | .24 | .10 | 6.2 | 0 |
| Bread, white, enriched (1 lb) | 1 loaf | 454 | 1,225 | 39 | 15 | 381 | 11.3 | trace | 1.13 | .95 | 10.9 | trace |
| Bread, whole wheat, firm (1 lb) | 1 loaf | 454 | 1,100 | 48 | 14 | 449 | 13.6 | trace | 1.18 | .54 | 12.7 | trace |
| Cornmeal, whole ground, unbolted, dry | 1 cup | 122 | 435 | 11 | 5 | 24 | 2.9 | 620 | .46 | .13 | 2.4 | 0 |
| Graham Crackers (2½ in. sq.) | 4 crackers | 28 | 110 | 2 | 3 | 11 | .4 | 0 | .01 | .06 | .4 | 0 |
| Macaroni, enriched, cooked, firm | 1 cup | 130 | 190 | 6 | 1 | 14 | 1.4 | 0 | .23 | .14 | 1.8 | 0 |
| Oatmeal or rolled oats, cooked | 1 cup | 240 | 130 | 5 | 2 | 22 | 1.4 | 0 | .19 | .05 | .2 | 0 |
| ²Rice, brown, cooked | 1 cup | 205 | 238 | 5 | 1 | 24 | 1.0 | 0 | .18 | .04 | 2.8 | 0 |
| Rice, white, enriched, cooked | 1 cup | 205 | 225 | 4 | trace | 21 | 1.8 | 0 | .23 | .02 | 2.1 | 0 |
| Whole wheat flour | 1 cup | 120 | 400 | 16 | 2 | 49 | 4.0 | 0 | .66 | .14 | 5.2 | 0 |
| White flour, enriched | 1 cup | 115 | 420 | 12 | 1 | 18 | 3.3 | 0 | .51 | .30 | 4.0 | 0 |
| ²Soybean flour, low fat (for comparison) | 1 cup | 120 | 425 | 52 | 8 | 315 | 10.9 | 96 | 1.00 | .42 | 3.1 | 0 |
| ²Wheat Germ, raw | 1 cup | 100 | 363 | 27 | 11 | 72 | 9.4 | 0 | 2.01 | .68 | 4.2 | 0 |

## FATS and OILS

| Food | Measure | | | | | | | | | | | |
|---|---|---|---|---|---|---|---|---|---|---|---|---|
| Butter, regular, stick | ½ cup | 113 | 810 | 1 | 92 | 23 | 0 | 3,750 | — | — | — | 0 |
| Cooking fats: lard | 1 cup | 205 | 1,850 | 0 | 205 | 0 | 0 | 0 | 0 | 0 | 0 | 0 |
| Vegetable fats | 1 cup | 200 | 1,770 | 0 | 200 | 0 | 0 | 0 | 0 | 0 | 0 | 0 |
| Margarine, regular, stick | ½ cup | 113 | 815 | 1 | 92 | 23 | 0 | 3,750 | — | — | — | 0 |
| Oils, safflower | 1 cup | 220 | 1,945 | 0 | 220 | 0 | 0 | 0 | 0 | 0 | 0 | 0 |
| Yeast, brewer's dry | 1 tbsp | 8 | 25 | 3 | trace | 17 | 1.4 | trace | 1.25 | .34 | 3.0 | trace |

¹Food value taken from: **Watt & Merrill, *Composition of Foods*; Washington, U.S.D.A., 1963**
²Food value taken from: *Fearn Chart*, Composition of Foods; © Fearn Soya Foods, Inc., Melrose Park, Illinois, 1961

# APPENDIX G
## RECOMMENDED READING

**Cookbooks:**

*International Vegetarian Cookery*; Sonya Richmond; Arco Publishing Co., New York, New York

*Meatless Cooking: Pegeen's Vegetarian Recipes*; Pegeen Fitzgerald; Prentiss Hall Inc., Englewood Cliffs, New Jersey

*New Age Vegetarian Cookbook*; Augusta Foss Heindel; The Rosicrucian Fellowship, Oceanside, California

*The New Unity Inn Cookbook*; Unity Books, Lee's Summit, Missouri

*Recipes for Vegetarians*; Mattie Louise Gephardt; Theosophical Publishing House, Wheaton, Illinois

*The Soybean Cookbook*; Dorothea Van Gundy Jones; Arc Books Inc., New York, New York

*Ten Talents*; Frank J. and Rosalie Hurd; Route 1, Chisholm, Minnesota

*The Vegan Kitchen*; Freya Dinshah; The American Vegan Society, Malaga, New Jersey

*Vegetarian Cookery*; Janet Walker; Wilshire Book Co., North Hollywood, California

*Vegetarian Gourmet Cookery*; Alan Hooker; 101 Productions, San Francisco, California

*Victory Through Vegetables*; Joan Wiener; Ballantine Books, New York, New York

**Additional Reading:**

*Diet for a Small Planet*; Frances Moore Lappé; Ballantine Books, New York, New York

## Scientific Nutrition

*About Food Values*; Barbara Davis; Thorsons Publishers Ltd., London, 1959

*Let's Eat Right to Keep Fit*; Adelle Davis; New American Library, New York, 1970

*Natural Hygiene Educator,* Vol. 2, No. 6, December 1969

*No Me, Know Me, No Meat*; Jon Dieges; published by the author

*Present Knowledge of Nutrition*; O. A. Roels; The Nutrition Foundation Inc., New York, 1967

*Radiant Health from a Meat Free Dietary*; Geoffrey Hodson; The New Zealand Vegetarian Society, Inc., Auckland

*Recommended Daily Allowances*; National Research Council, Food and Nutrition Board, National Academy of Sciences, Washington, D.C., 1965, p. 102

*Superior Nutrition*; Herbert M. Shelton; Dr. Shelton's Health School, San Antonio, 1965

*Why Kill For Food?*; Geoffrey Rudd; The Vegetarian Society, Cheshire, England, 1956

# INDEX

For a complete descriptive list of all Quest Books
write to:

QUEST BOOKS
P.O. Box 270, Wheaton, IL 60187